MR 01 '04	DATE DUE		

AIDS

William A. Check

Introduction by C. Everett Koop, M.D., Sc.D.
Former Surgeon General, U.S. Public Health Service

Foreword by Sandra Thurman
Director, Office of National AIDS Policy, The White House

CHELSEA HOUSE PUBLISHERS
Philadelphia

The goal of the ENCYCLOPEDIA OF HEALTH is to provide general information in the ever changing areas of physiology, psychology, and related medical issues. The titles in this series are not intended to take the place of the professional advice of a physician or other health-care professional.

Chelsea House Publishers
EDITOR-IN-CHIEF: Stephen Reginald
PRODUCTION MANAGER: Pam Loos
ART DIRECTOR: Sara Davis
DIRECTOR OF PHOTOGRAPHY: Judy Hasday
MANAGING EDITOR: James D. Gallagher
SENIOR PRODUCTION EDITOR: J. Christopher Higgins
ASSISTANT EDITOR: Anne Hill
PRODUCTION SERVICES: Pre-Press Company, Inc.

Staff for AIDS
SENIOR EDITOR: Jane Larkin Crain
ASSISTANT EDITOR: James Cornelius
COPY EDITOR: Karen Hammonds
DEPUTY COPY CHIEF: Ellen Scordato
EDITORIAL ASSISTANTS: Nicole Bowen, Susan DeRosa
ASSOCIATE PICTURE EDITOR: Juliette Dickstein
PICTURE RESEARCHER: Villette Harris
DESIGN: Debby Jay, Jean Weiss
DESIGNER: Victoria Tomaselli
PRODUCTION COORDINATOR: Joseph Romano

Staff for AIDS update
RESEARCHER: Petra Press
SENIOR EDITOR: James D. Gallagher
EDITORIAL ASSISTANT: Anne Hill
ASSOCIATE ART DIRECTOR: Takeshi Takahashi
DESIGNER: Brian Wible
COVER DESIGNER/ILLUSTRATOR: Emiliano Begnardi

The Chelsea House World Wide Web address is http://www.chelseahouse.com

5 7 9 8 6 4

Library of Congress Cataloging in Publication Data
Check, William A.
AIDS
(21st Century health and wellness)
Bibliography: p.
Includes index
1. AIDS (Diseases)—Popular works. I. Title. II. Series.
RC607.A26C48   1988   616.9'792   87-34101
ISBN 0-7910-4885-3

CONTENTS

Prevention and Education: The Keys to Good Health—
C. Everett Koop, M.D., Sc.D.   5

Foreword—
Sandra Thurman, Director, Office of National AIDS Policy,
The White House   11

1   A Twentieth-Century Plague   13

2   Sounding the First Alarm   19

3   The Epidemic Explodes   33

4   Identifying the Virus   51

5   Helping the Victims   57

6   The Fight Against Aids   67

7   Public Response to the Disease   73

8   Encouraging Treatment Breakthroughs   87

9   Protecting Yourself from Aids   103

10 Conclusion   111

Appendix: For More Information   115

Further Reading   118

Aids Hotlines   119

Glossary   120

Index   123

- **AIDS**
- **Allergies**
- **The Circulatory System**
- **The Common Cold**
- **Death & Dying**
- **The Digestive System**
- **The Endocrine System**
- **Headaches**
- **Holistic Medicine**
- **The Human Body: An Overview**
- **The Immune System**
- **Mononucleosis and Other Infectious Diseases**
- **Organ Transplants**
- **Pregnancy & Birth**
- **The Respiratory System**
- **Sexually Transmitted Diseases**
- **Skin Disorders**
- **Sports Medicine**
- **Stress Management**

PREVENTION AND EDUCATION: THE KEYS TO GOOD HEALTH

C. Everett Koop, M.D., Sc.D.
FORMER SURGEON GENERAL,
U.S. Public Health Service

The issue of health education has received particular attention in recent years because of the presence of AIDS in the news. But our response to this particular tragedy points up a number of broader issues that doctors, public health officials, educators, and the public face. In particular, it spotlights the importance of sound health education for citizens of all ages.

Over the past 35 years, this country has been able to achieve dramatic declines in the death rates from heart disease, stroke, accidents, and—for people under the age of 45—cancer. Today, Americans generally eat better and take better care of themselves than ever before. Thus, with the help of modern science and technology, they have a better chance of surviving serious—even catastrophic—illnesses. In 1996, the life expectancy of Americans reached an all-time high of 76.1 years. That's the good news.

The flip side of this advance has special significance for young adults. According to a report issued in 1998 by the U.S. Department of Health and Human Services, levels of wealth and education in the United States are directly correlated with our population's health. The more money Americans make and the more years of schooling they have, the better their health will be. Furthermore, income inequality increased in the U.S. between 1970 and 1996. Basically, the rich got richer—people in high income brackets had greater increases in the amount of money made than did those at low income levels. In addition, the report indicated that children under 18 are more likely to live in poverty than the population as a whole.

Family income rises with each higher level of education for both men and women from every ethnic and racial background. Life expectancy, too, is related to family income. People with lower incomes tend to die at younger ages than people from more affluent homes. What all this means is that health is a factor of wealth and education, both of which need to be improved for all Americans if the promise of life, liberty, and the pursuit of happiness is to include an equal chance for good health.

The health of young people is further threatened by violent death and injury, alcohol and drug abuse, unwanted pregnancies, and sexually transmitted diseases. Adolescents are particularly vulnerable because they are beginning to explore their own sexuality and perhaps to experiment with drugs and alcohol. We need to educate young people to avoid serious dangers to their health. The price of neglect is high.

Even for the population as a whole, health is still far from what it could be. Why? Most death and disease are attributed to four broad elements: inadequacies in the health-care system, behavioral factors or unhealthy lifestyles, environmental hazards, and human biological factors. These categories are also influenced by individual resources. For example, low birth weight and infant mortality are more common among the children of less educated mothers. Likewise, women with more education are more likely to obtain prenatal care during pregnancy. Mothers with fewer than 12 years of education are almost 10 times more likely to smoke during pregnancy—and new studies find excessive aggression later in life as well as other physical ailments among the children of smokers. In short, poor people with less education are more likely to smoke cigarettes, which endangers health and shortens the life span. About a third of the children who begin smoking will eventually have their lives cut short because of this practice.

Similarly, poor children are exposed more often to environmental lead, which causes a wide range of physical and mental problems. Sedentary lifestyles are also more common among teens with lower family income than among wealthier adolescents. Being overweight—a condition associated with physical inactivity as well as excessive caloric intake—is also more common among poor, non-Hispanic, white adolescents. Children from rich families are more likely to have health insurance. Therefore, they are more apt to receive vaccinations and other forms of early preventative medicine and treatment. The bottom line is that kids from lower income groups receive less adequate health care.

To be sure, some diseases are still beyond the control of even the most advanced medical techniques that our richest citizens can afford. Despite yearnings that are as old as the human race itself, there is no "fountain of youth" to prevent aging and death. Still, solutions are available for many of the problems that undermine sound health. In a word, that solution is prevention. Prevention, which includes health promotion and education, can save lives, improve the quality of life, and, in the long run, save money.

In the United States, organized public health activities and preventative medicine have a long history. Important milestones include the improvement of sanitary procedures and the development of pasteurized milk in the late-19th century, and the introduction in the mid-20th century of effective vaccines against polio, measles, German measles, mumps, and other once-rampant diseases. Internationally, organized public health efforts began on a wide-scale basis with the International Sanitary Conference of 1851, to which 12 nations sent representatives. The World Health Organization, founded in 1948, continues these efforts under the aegis of the United Nations, with particular emphasis on combating communicable diseases and the training of health-care workers.

Despite these accomplishments, much remains to be done in the field of prevention. For too long, we have had a medical system that is science and technology-based, and focuses essentially on illness and mortality. It is now patently obvious that both the social and the economic costs of such a system are becoming insupportable.

Implementing prevention and its corollaries, health education and health promotion, is the job of several groups of people. First, the medical and scientific professions need to continue basic scientific research, and here we are making considerable progress. But increased concern with prevention will also have a decided impact on how primary-care doctors practice medicine. With a shift to health-based rather than morbidity-based medicine, the role of the "new physician" includes a healthy dose of patient education.

Second, practitioners of the social and behavioral sciences—psychologists, economists, and city planners along with lawyers, business leaders, and government officials—must solve the practical and ethical dilemmas confronting us: poverty, crime, civil rights, literacy, education, employment, housing, sanitation, environmental protection, health-care delivery systems, and so forth. All of these issues affect public health.

Third is the public at large. We consider this group to be important in any movement. Fourth, and the linchpin in this effort, is the public health profession: doctors, epidemiologists, teachers—who must harness the professional expertise of the first two groups and the common sense and cooperation of the third: the public. They must define the problems statistically and qualitatively and then help set priorities for finding solutions.

To a very large extent, improving health statistics is the responsibility of every individual. So let's consider more specifically what the role of the individual should be and why health education is so important. First, and most obviously, individuals can protect themselves from illness and injury and thus minimize the need for professional medical care. They can eat a nutritious diet; get adequate exercise; avoid tobacco, alcohol, and drugs; and take prudent steps to avoid accidents. The proverbial "apple a day keeps the doctor away" is not so far from the truth, after all.

Second, individuals should actively participate in their own medical care. They should schedule regular medical and dental checkups. If an illness or injury develops, they should know when to treat themselves and when to seek professional help. To gain the maximum benefit from any medical treatment, individuals must become partners in treatment. For instance, they should understand the effects and side effects of medications. I counsel young physicians that there is no such thing as too much information when talking with patients. But the corollary is the patient must know enough about the nuts and bolts of the healing process to understand what the doctor is telling him or her. That responsibility is at least partially the patient's.

Education is equally necessary for us to understand the ethical and public policy issues in health care today. Sometimes individuals will encounter these issues in making decisions about their own treatment or that of family members. Other citizens may encounter them as jurors in medical malpractice cases. But we all become involved, indirectly, when we elect our public officials, from school board members to the president. Should surrogate parenting be legal? To what extent is drug testing desirable, legal, or necessary? Should there be public funding for family planning, hospitals, various types of medical research, and medical care for the indigent? How should we allocate scant technological resources, such as kidney dialysis and organ transplants? What is the proper role of government in protecting the rights of patients?

What are the broad goals of public health in the United States today? The Public Health Service has defined these goals in terms of mortality, education, and health improvement. It identified 15 major concerns: controlling high blood pressure, improving family planning, pregnancy care and infant health, increasing the rate of immunization, controlling sexually transmitted diseases, controlling the presence of toxic agents or radiation in the environment, improving occupational safety and health, preventing accidents, promoting water fluoridation and dental health, controlling infectious diseases, decreasing smoking, decreasing alcohol and drug abuse, improving nutrition, promoting physical fitness and exercise, and controlling stress and violent behavior. Great progress has been made in many of these areas. For example, the report *Health, United States, 1998* indicates that in general, the workplace is safer today than it was a decade ago. Between 1980 and 1993, the overall death rate from occupational injuries dropped 45 percent to 4.2 deaths per 100,000 workers.

For healthy adolescents and young adults (ages 15 to 24), the specific goal defined by the Public Health Service was a 20% reduction in deaths, with a special focus on motor vehicle injuries as well as alcohol and drug abuse. For adults (ages 25 to 64), the aim was 25% fewer deaths, with a concentration on heart attacks, strokes, and cancers. In the 1999 National Drug Control Strategy, the White House Office of National Drug Control Policy echoed the Congressional goal of reducing drug use by 50 percent in the coming decade.

Smoking is perhaps the best example of how individual behavior can have a direct impact on health. Today cigarette smoking is recognized as the most important single preventable cause of death in our society. It is responsible for more cancers and more cancer deaths than any other known agent; is a prime risk factor for heart and blood vessel disease, chronic bronchitis, and emphysema; and is a frequent cause of complications in pregnancies and of babies born prematurely, underweight, or with potentially fatal respiratory and cardiovascular problems.

Since the release of the Surgeon General's first report on smoking in 1964, the proportion of adult smokers has declined substantially, from 43% in 1965 to 30.5% in 1985. The rate of cigarette smoking among adults declined from 1974 to 1995, but rates of decline were greater among the more educated. Since 1965, more than 50 million people have quit smoking. Although the rate of adult smoking has decreased, children and teenagers are smoking more. Researchers have also noted a disturbing correlation between underage smoking of cigarettes and later use of cocaine and heroin. Although there is still much work to be done if we are to become a "smoke free society," it is heartening to note that public health and public education efforts—such as warnings on cigarette packages, bans on broadcast advertising, removal of billboards advertising cigarettes, and anti-drug youth campaigns in the media—have already had significant effects.

In 1997, the first leveling off of drug use since 1992 was found in eighth graders, with marijuana use in the past month declining to 10 percent. The percentage of eighth graders who drink alcohol or smoke cigarettes also decreased slightly in 1997. In 1994 and 1995, there were more than 142,000 cocaine-related emergency-room episodes per year, the highest number ever reported since these events were tracked starting in 1978. Illegal drugs present a serious threat to Americans who use these drugs. Addiction is a chronic, relapsing disease that changes the chemistry of the brain in harmful ways. The abuse of inhalants and solvents found in legal products like hair spray, paint thinner, and industrial cleaners—called "huffing" (through the mouth) or "sniffing" (through the nose)—has come to public attention in recent years. *The National Household Survey on Drug Abuse* discovered that among youngsters ages 12 to 17, this dangerous practice doubled between 1991 and 1996 from 10.3 percent to 21 percent. An alarming large number of children died the very first time they tried inhalants, which can also cause brain damage or injure other vital organs.

Another threat to public health comes from firearm injuries. Fortunately, the number of such assaults declined between 1993 and 1996. Nevertheless, excessive violence in our culture—as depicted in the mass media—may have contributed to the random shootings at Columbine High School in Littleton, Colorado, and elsewhere. The government and private citizens are rethinking how to reduce the fascination with violence so that America can become a safer, healthier place to live.

The "smart money" is on improving health care for everyone. Only recently did we realize that the gap between the "haves" and "have-nots" had a significant health component. One more reason to invest in education is that schooling produces better health.

In 1835, Alexis de Tocqueville, a French visitor to America, wrote, "In America, the passion for physical well-being is general." Today, as then, health and fitness are front-page items. But with the greater scientific and technological resources now available to us, we are in a far stronger position to make good health care available to everyone. With the greater technological threats to us as we approach the 21st century, the need to do so is more urgent than ever before. Comprehensive information about basic biology, preventative medicine, medical and surgical treatments, and related ethical and public policy issues can help you arm yourself with adequate knowledge to be healthy throughout life.

**Sandra Thurman, Director, Office of National AIDS Policy,
The White House**

A hundred years ago, an era was marked by discovery, invention, and the infinite possibilities of progress. Nothing piqued society's curiosity more than the mysterious workings of the human body. They poked and prodded, experimented with new remedies and discarded old ones, increased longevity and reduced death rates. But not even the most enterprising minds of the day could have dreamed of the advancements that would soon become our shared reality. Could they have envisioned that we would vaccinate millions of children against polio? Ward off the annoyance of allergy season with a single pill? Or give life to a heart that had stopped keeping time?

As we stand on the brink of a new millennium, the progress made during the last hundred years is indeed staggering. And we continue to push forward every minute of every day. We now exist in a working global community, blasting through cyber-space at the speed of light, sharing knowledge and up-to-the-minute technology. We are in a unique position to benefit from the world's rich fabric of traditional healing practices while continuing to explore advances in modern medicine. In the halls of our medical schools, tomorrow's healers are learning to appreciate the complexities of our whole person. We are not only keeping people alive, we are keeping them well.

Although we deserve to rejoice in our progress, we must also remember that our health remains a complex web. Our world changes with each step forward and we are continuously faced with new threats to our well-being. The air we breathe has become polluted, the water tainted, and new killers have emerged to challenge us in ways we are just beginning to understand. AIDS, in particular, continues to tighten its grip on America's most fragile communities, and place our next generation in jeopardy.

Facing these new challenges will require us to find inventive ways to stay healthy. We already know the dangers of alcohol, smoking and drug abuse. We also understand the benefits of early detection for illnesses like cancer and heart disease, two areas where scientists have made significant in-roads to treatment. We have become a well-informed society, and with that information comes a renewed emphasis on preventative care and a sense of personal responsibility to care for both ourselves and those who need our help.

Read. Re-read. Study. Explore the amazing working machine that is the human body. Share with your friends and your families what you have learned. It is up to all of us living together as a community to care for our well-being, and to continue working for a healthier quality of life.

CHAPTER 1

A TWENTIETH-CENTURY PLAGUE

The mounting toll acquired immunodeficiency syndrome, or AIDS, has taken on U.S. families was illustrated dramatically in October 1996, when relatives and friends of those who have died of the disease visited a mile-long Memorial Quilt. The quilt is made of individual panels about six feet by three feet, each representing a victim of AIDS. It was sewn into groups of eight panels and divided between pathways so visitors could see the individual tributes. First shown in 1987, by the time the quilt was displayed in 1996 it had grown to honor the memories of 70,000 AIDS fatalities. While most of those remembered are Americans, the dead of 39 other countries are also in the quilt, including Germans, Cubans, Italians, Japanese, Russians, Venezuelans, and Zambians.

Some of the hand-sewn panels just give the victim's name, birth and death dates, and perhaps a portrait or photograph. Others include personal items such as a passport, a pair of jeans, a teddy bear, or a poem. For many who visited the display, AIDS became, for the first time, a poignant tragedy of names and faces, not just numbers.

Forty years ago there was tremendous excitement about the first wonder drugs, penicillin and other newly discovered antibiotics. These medicines cured patients of many bacterial infections that previously had been fatal. One medical journalist, Berton Roueché, visited a laboratory where researchers were searching for more potent antibiotics. In a burst of enthusiasm over this triumph of modern medical science, he wrote: "[A]s I gathered during my tour of the laboratories, it is not impossible that the present broad and energetic search for new antibiotics will lead within the next few years to the discovery of microbial antagonists capable of hobbling all infectious disease."

It has not happened. Today, despite the continuing production of

Engraving of London during the Plague of 1665. The AIDS epidemic has been compared to some of history's most devastating disease outbreaks.

better antibiotics since the discovery of penicillin, we are facing an infectious disease against which all these drugs are virtually powerless. This disease, AIDS, is spreading inexorably, killing more and more people each year. AIDS knows no national boundaries and does not discriminate by race or sex. It is rampaging not only through the United States, but also through Africa, India, China, Russia, Europe, South America, and the Caribbean countries. Even infants and children are at risk.

One observer has called AIDS "unique in the annals of medicine." That is not quite true. AIDS has parallels in medical history, but they are very disturbing ones. AIDS can be compared to the epidemics of small-pox that ravaged the world for thousands of years before its eradication in the late 1970s. AIDS is also similar in some ways to the bubonic plague, the "Black Death" that killed perhaps one-third of the people in Europe in the 14th century. One scientist has spoken of AIDS as "the Black Death in slow motion," because the infectious agent that causes AIDS can remain dormant in a person's body for several years before it causes illness, and because death from AIDS can be slow and drawn out once symptoms appear.

A DEADLY DISEASE

AIDS is essentially a disease of the immune system. The body's defenses are destroyed and the patient becomes prey to infections and cancers that would normally be fought off without any trouble. In 1984 it was proved that AIDS is caused by the human immunodeficiency virus (HIV). A virus is a minute infectious particle that enters and kills the immune cells, or lymphocytes.

Because it destroys the very mechanisms humans rely on for protection, prior to 1996 contracting AIDS was considered a death sentence. For many years, 85 to 90 percent of all AIDS patients died within three years. They might have recovered from one infection only to succumb to another a few months later. Between infections they remained weak, emaciated, and unable to work or carry on normal activities.

In late 1996, almost 15 years after the first reported AIDS cases, researchers made the discovery that a certain combination of newly developed drugs could substantially prolong life in some AIDS patients. But AIDS is a fiendish virus. When researchers successfully cleared it out of a patient's bloodstream, it hid in the lymph nodes. When the scientists figured out how to banish it from the lymph nodes, they found the virus lurking in the brain.

Also in 1996, other researchers isolated a gene that appears to protect some people from HIV infection, even after repeated exposure. Their experiments may lead to new genetic therapies against AIDS. For the first time in 15 years there is hope for a cure, but even with the exciting recent developments in drug treatment, there is neither a cure for AIDS nor a vaccine to immunize people against HIV infection.

The worldwide scope of this epidemic is staggering. According to Dr. Peter Lamptey, director of the AIDS Control and Prevention Project, epidemiologists tracking AIDS report the largest area of concern is Southeast Asia—particularly India. At 900 million, India's population is almost double that of sub-Saharan Africa, which, with 13.3 million HIV-positive adults, accounts for 60 percent of the world's total adult infections.

In late 1996, researchers estimated that at least five million people in India have been infected with the HIV virus. Because no reliable figures have been compiled, it is impossible to make an accurate prediction of how AIDS will spread there; however, India's huge population, high poverty rate, and other risk factors all point to a likely explosion. So far, the pattern is similar to that of Africa at the start of the epidemic.

In October 1996, according to a study on the spread of the disease sponsored by the United Nations, Harvard, and the AIDS Control and Prevention Project, the number of HIV infections worldwide doubled between 1991 and 1996—and that number is expected to double again by the year 2000. By the turn of the century, about 44 million people will have fallen victim to the virus that causes AIDS, up from an estimated 21.8 million in 1996, according to projections released at the 11th International Conference on AIDS. Dr. Daniel Tarantola, director of the International AIDS Program at the Harvard School of Public Health, said the number of AIDS infections could climb as high as 70 million, depending on the course of the disease.

But the researchers also said there were signs of hope that the relentless spread of AIDS could be stopped. Prevention programs have succeeded in reducing HIV-infection rates dramatically among young men in Thailand and young women in Uganda—two of the countries hit hardest by the disease. The rate of new infections also has dropped sharply among gay men in the United States, Australia, Canada, and western Europe.

Protests by parents, who feared their children would catch AIDS from infected schoolmates, have been part of the public outcry against the disease. However, AIDS cannot be spread by casual contact in school.

However, many ingredients of the AIDS epidemic are still a mystery. The cause of AIDS remained uncertain for several years after its discovery. Even now, there are questions about how efficiently the AIDS virus spreads, whether it will kill everyone who gets it, and why the virus is so devastating to the immune system.

In addition, AIDS has caused social upheaval. Because its initial spread in the United States was among groups that are frowned upon by society—homosexuals and intravenous (IV) drug users—AIDS has a stigma associated with it. This makes the disease difficult to confront rationally.

Dr. Peter Sandman of Rutgers University has found that people's fear of getting a disease becomes most intense when the ways of acquiring that disease involve behavior that may have moral overtones. Homosexuality and drug abuse are considered morally wrong by many people in our society. As a result, people with AIDS and those who have tested HIV-positive are often ostracized by the community, even when they are not homosexuals or drug users. In several cases, children who contracted AIDS through contaminated blood transfusions became the target of angry parents, who demanded they be banned from school because they feared their own children would "catch" the disease from an infected classmate. Many religious groups objected when educators and concerned parents proposed the distribution of condoms to young people as part of an AIDS education program. Even a number of doctors and dentists publicly refused to treat AIDS patients.

However, the disease does not pass from one person to another through the air, by sneezing, on eating utensils, by shaking hands, or through body contact in sports. There are only four ways it can be spread: through injection with a needle contaminated with HIV, which can happen when drug addicts share needles; by having sex with a person who is infected with the virus; by receiving a transfusion of contaminated blood; or—in the case of an infant with an HIV-positive mother—having the virus transmitted through the placenta before birth, or through the mother's milk after birth.

For years, some people refused to admit AIDS was a problem. Although the disease first received national attention in 1981, when the Centers for Disease Control (CDC) noticed an alarming rate of a rare cancer (Kaposi's sarcoma) in otherwise healthy gay men, President Ronald Reagan did not publicly mention the disease until six years later—long after the FDA approved the first HIV antibody test, the first International Conference on AIDS had been held, U.S. Surgeon General C. Everett Koop had called for a national sex education program, and celebrities such as Rock Hudson made headlines with AIDS-related deaths. (In 1990, after he left office, Reagan officially apologized for neglecting the epidemic while in the White House.)

Ignoring the problem or responding with anger and fear makes the struggle to cope with this terrible disease even more difficult. Understanding how to avoid contracting AIDS is especially important for young people, who will spend their lives with the threat of the disease. Communities, schools, church groups, and political groups all must work together to accomplish this task. It is equally important for countries to work together to overcome AIDS on a global level.

At the same time, the best possible care must be made available to AIDS patients and their loved ones. Also, full support must be given to research efforts to eradicate the disease.

CHAPTER 2

SOUNDING THE FIRST ALARM

Dr. Michael Gottlieb

Between December 1980 and March 1981, Dr. Michael Gottlieb of the University of California–Los Angeles (UCLA) Medical Center, was called in to consult on three puzzling patients. Dr. Gottlieb, a specialist in the immune system, the body's defense against foreign invaders, often saw patients who were quite sick with an uncommon ailment.

As expected, the three patients Dr. Gottlieb examined were very ill. Interestingly, they had several striking features in common. All had unusual infections such as thrush, which is the growth in the throat of a fungus called *Candida*; or a rare type of pneumonia caused by a parasite called *Pneumocystis*. Also, they had all been infected by less-common viruses, such as

Epstein-Barr virus, which causes mononucleosis, or by cytomegalovirus (CMV). Taken together, the infections pointed to a serious defect in the patients' immune systems.

Sure enough, when Dr. Gottlieb drew a vial of blood from each patient and measured a special kind of immune cell called a *T-helper lymphocyte*, all three patients' tests gave the same startling result. "They were virtually devoid of T-helper cells," Dr. Gottlieb found. It was clear that they had seriously deficient immune systems.

The three men had something else in common: they were all homosexuals. At that time it was not clear that the patients' homosexuality was related to the illness; a patient's sexual preference had never before been considered the determining factor of a medical disorder. That situation was about to change radically.

Dr. Gottlieb had identified the patients' basic problem as an acquired immune deficiency. (*Acquired* refers to the fact that they had not been born with the lack of immunity.) But even with his special knowledge, Dr. Gottlieb could not diagnose the source of their problem. Lacking insight into the root cause of the patients' illness, the UCLA doctors could only fight the infections as best they knew how, with the available antibiotics. However, in patients without their own natural defenses, antibiotics lose their potency. All three patients died.

Intrigued by these cases, Dr. Gottlieb spoke to a colleague in the Los Angeles City Health Department who uncovered another patient that fit the description: a gay man in Santa Monica with a CMV infection who had recently died of *pneumocystis* pneumonia. A fifth case soon turned up, and Dr. Gottlieb knew that something mysterious but significant was happening.

THE EARLY DETECTIVE WORK

Although Dr. Gottlieb could not have known it at the time, he was seeing the first manifestations of what would become the AIDS epidemic. What he did next was crucial in alerting government health officials to this emerging public-health threat. He sent a report about the five patients to Atlanta, Georgia, to a government agency called the Centers for Disease Control, or CDC, part of the Public Health Service.

The CDC is the federal government's lead agency for tracking down disease outbreaks, or epidemics. The heart of the CDC's staff is a corps of epidemiologists, physician-scientists who are trained to trace a

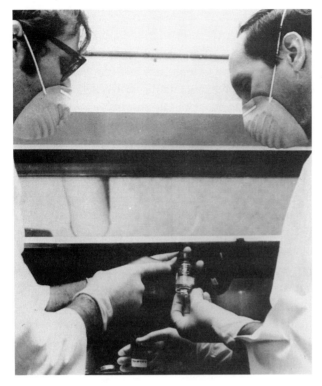

Doctors at the Centers for Disease Control in Atlanta, which has taken a leading role in trying to stop the spread of AIDS in the United States since the start of the epidemic.

disease outbreak to its source. These epidemiologists have popularly been called disease detectives. CDC workers are often assigned to small, localized health problems, such as transmission of hepatitis from contaminated cream doughnuts or of diarrhea from raw milk.

The Centers have tackled major disease outbreaks as well. It was epidemiologists and scientists from the CDC who investigated the outbreak of Legionnaires' disease at a hotel in Philadelphia in 1976 and identified the source of the infection. CDC personnel played a major role in the worldwide smallpox eradication campaign. Also, in 1980, the year before AIDS appeared, CDC scientists defined Toxic Shock Syndrome and discovered that it was often caused by tampons.

So when Dr. Gottlieb alerted the CDC to the five unusual cases he had seen, the CDC immediately began thinking on a national scale. Phone calls went out to physicians and public-health departments across the country. In New York City they hit pay dirt.

At the Sloan-Kettering Cancer Center, Dr. Donald Armstrong and Dr. Jon Gold said they had seen a number of cases similar to those seen by Dr. Gottlieb. Some patients had CMV infection, others had *pneumo-cystis* pneumonia. In some patients there was infection of the brain called *toxoplasmosis*, caused by the parasite *Toxoplasma*. Others had severe, uncontrollable ulcers around the anus caused by herpes virus. Usually, a bad cold sore is the worst sign of herpes virus in a healthy person (though genital herpes is more severe). But in these men the herpes infections were spreading throughout the body.

The Sloan-Kettering physicians verified with laboratory tests that their patients, too, had a severe deficiency in immunity. And when alerted by the CDC to the sexual orientation of the Los Angeles patients, the Sloan-Kettering doctors went back to find out their patients' status. They were indeed homosexual.

The attacking microorganisms seen in these patients are rarely a problem in otherwise healthy people. They were taking advantage of a breach in the immune system to invade the body, which is why they are called *opportunistic infections.* Cancer patients are treated with drugs that also damage the immune system, so Dr. Armstrong and Dr. Gold were used to seeing opportunistic infections. But even they were surprised by the severity of the illnesses seen in the gay men. "We didn't know what to make of it," Dr. Gold said.

KAPOSI'S SARCOMA

If the infectious disease specialists were puzzled, several New York dermatologists were even more perplexed. These doctors, who specialize in skin diseases, were seeing a number of patients with an extremely rare kind of cancer called *Kaposi's sarcoma.* Usually this cancer first becomes visible as dark red or violet blotches on the skin. Often when a patient is found to have a Kaposi's spot on the skin, further examination reveals the presence of the cancer in an internal organ, such as the stomach, as well.

Kaposi's sarcoma is so rare that many dermatologists would not even recognize it, but it suddenly began appearing it in New York City men. Moreover, it was showing up in men with the wrong characteristics. Kaposi's sarcoma had been a disease of elderly men of Mediterranean origin; in New York City it began to appear in young men of every ethnic background. It had been known as a slow-growing cancer that could be treated successfully; in these new, young patients the sarcoma was spreading fast and damaging internal organs.

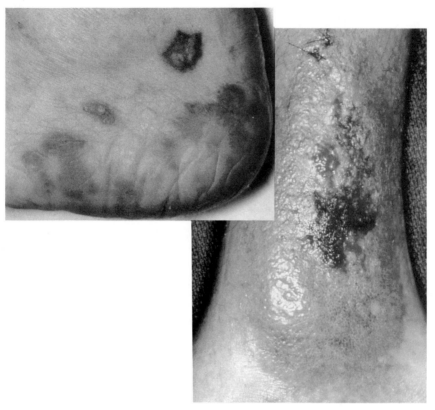

Skin lesions symptomatic of Kaposi's Sarcoma on a heel (above) and an ankle (right). Kaposi's Sarcoma, common in AIDS victims, is an otherwise rare skin cancer that signals a profound deficiency in the immune system.

The New York City doctors had been seeing young men with Kaposi's sarcoma for a year or two before Dr. Gottlieb's report to the CDC, but each doctor had seen only one or two such patients, not enough to attract anyone's attention for long. Then the CDC investigators began calling doctors and asking them whether they had seen any young, gay patients with opportunistic infections. No, they had not, they said, but they had seen some young gay men with Kaposi's sarcoma. It began to look as though the Kaposi's patients were part of a larger picture.

A cancer of the skin and internal organs does not sound like it would be related to rare infections of the lung and brain. But there is a strong connection—the immune system. It is one of the principles of the science of immunology that immune cells are essential in protecting the body from tumor cells. If a small colony of cancer cells, a tumor,

SIGNS AND SYMPTOMS OF AIDS

Early symptoms of HIV, lasting between one and four weeks, can mimic that of mononucleosis, with symptoms such as swelling of the lymph nodes, headache, fever, loss of appetite, weight loss, sweating, and sore throat. Often these symptoms are mistaken for the flu or another viral-type infection, so people may not even be aware they have been infected with HIV. Even if the patient has seen a doctor, the physician may dismiss the symptoms as a viral infection. In nearly all cases, this stage dissipates due to the healthy immune system's ability to fight the initial infection. Early symptoms also can include:

- Herpes zoster (shingles), a skin rash that can appear on the chest, abdomen, and/or back.

- Herpes simplex, a common sexually transmitted disease that affects the rectal, genital, and esophageal regions of the body. Painful lesions can erupt into ulcerations of the area. In HIV/AIDS patients, this may become a chronic condition.

- Thrush, a white coating on the walls of the mouth, gums, and on the tongue, that is caused by a fungus called *candida albicans*.

- Excessive bruising and bleeding that occurs when a person develops antibodies which attack the body's platelets—cells which help blood to clot. This condition can go unnoticed, and is often not detected until a routine blood test is performed.

- Chronic or intermittent diarrhea, found both in early and late stages of HIV infection.

As the immune system becomes increasingly compromised, the body is not able to fight off more serious infections that a normal intact immune system could suppress. Some of these life-threatening infections include:

- *Pneumocystis* pneumonia (PCP), caused by a parasite called *pneumocystis carinii*. Symptoms include fever and respiratory complications that often lead to death.

- Kaposi's sarcoma, a condition in which tumors of the blood vessels develop on the skin, in the gastrointestinal tract, mouth, lungs, groin, brain, liver, and lymph glands. The small, nonpainful lesions usually are a red, brown, or purple color.

- Tuberculosis (TB), which can occur in both early and late stages of HIV. Symptoms include night sweats, fever, cough, and weight loss. One of the major problems with this aspect of the disease is the development of TB strains resistant to drugs, making it harder and harder to treat.

- Mycobacterium avium complex, which produces fatigue, chills, night sweats, fever, weight loss, diarrhea, and abdominal pain.

- HIV-related lymphoma, swollen lymph glands in the neck, groin region, or under the arms. This requires radiation and chemotherapy treatment.

- Toxoplasmosis encephalitis, caused by a parasite, which produces an infection in the brain leading to neurological impairment and seizures. Symptoms include headaches, fevers, lethargy, confusion, and loss of balance or coordination.

- Cytomegalovirus (CMV) infection, a viral infection distributed to all parts of the body through the bloodstream and causing infections in the eyes, lungs, and other organs. About 90 percent of AIDS patients eventually develop cytomegalovirus.

- Cryptococcosis, produced by a fungus found in the soil. This causes a brain infection. Symptoms include fatigue, fever, nausea and vomiting, altered mental state, memory loss, confusion, and behavioral changes.

- Cryptosporidosis, an infection developed by drinking contaminated water, produces severe diarrhea and weight loss.

Dr. James Curran, the former director of the CDC AIDS branch, was one of the first people to track the epidemic.

becomes established, lymphocytes (part of the immune system) are supposed to find it and destroy it before it can grow. So Kaposi's sarcoma in these young gay men could be seen as an opportunistic cancer, taking advantage of the breakdown in the patients' defenses, just as the infectious organisms were doing.

There also was a more concrete reason for the doctors to know that the cases of Kaposi's sarcoma in young gay men signaled a breach of these persons' protective mechanisms: Kaposi's is relatively common in patients whose immune systems were suppressed by medical treatment. Patients who receive kidney transplants are treated with drugs to suppress the immune system so that the new kidney will not be destroyed by the immune cells before it has a chance to become established. The drugs used to treat cancer also knock out the immune system temporarily. Kaposi's sarcoma is often seen in both these types of patients.

Patients taking drugs that suppress the immune system are also prone to lymphoma, or cancer of the immune system. Soon this cancer started showing up in gay men, too.

WHY HOMOSEXUALS?

From the beginning, it was strikingly clear that the disease that was to be called AIDS was first and foremost a disorder of the immune system. That was a central fact that had to be explained by any theory of the cause of the disease.

What the doctors were seeing made sense, medically: patients who had grossly deficient immunity, and infectious agents and cancers that were taking advantage of this breakdown. But in a social context these cases raised a perplexing question: why were the illnesses almost exclusively striking homosexual men? From the start there was a suspicion that the answer had to do with sexual lifestyles.

Dr. James Curran, a CDC specialist, took part in the AIDS investigation from the beginning. He was designated the leader of the task force that started to track the epidemic in early 1981, and he later became director of the CDC's AIDS Branch. Dr. Curran recalled his reaction to the early reports of unusual diseases in gay men: "We had just been working with two other diseases that are very common in homosexual men and that are sexually transmitted—hepatitis B and gonorrhea. So our first thought was that the occurrence of *pneumocystis* pneumonia and Kaposi's sarcoma in homosexual men might involve sexual transmission."

Dr. Curran's statement implied two things. One, that there was an infectious organism underlying the unusual diseases (perhaps an infectious organism that attacked the immune system). Two, that the homosexual lifestyle was somehow unique. It would be three years before the suspicion of an infectious agent that attacked immune cells was verified by the isolation of the AIDS virus. But it was already known that gay men's sexual habits differed from those of most heterosexuals.

The story of homosexual awareness goes back to 1969, to a police raid on a gay disco in New York called Stonewall. At that time homosexual men were usually not open about their sexual preference—they were still "in the closet." They were often harassed by the police. But when New York City police raided Stonewall it turned out to be the last straw for many gays. They fought back, and riots ensued.

Within a few days a more constructive response was formulated—a parade openly celebrating "gay pride" that signaled the emergence of many homosexual men from the closet. And when they "came out"—publicly declared their homosexuality—one of the things many of them did was to throw themselves furiously into a sexually hyperactive lifestyle.

Two Studies on Sexual Practices: To appreciate the extent of this sexual liberation, we can look at the results of two case-control studies done during the early phase of the AIDS epidemic. The concept of a case-control study is simple: By asking a number of questions of people who have a disease and of similar people who do not, researchers can determine how they differ. Those differences are the clues to why certain people got sick and the others did not. For instance, if some people at a picnic get food poisoning and others do not, the study might ask whether most of the ill ones ate the potato salad. If so, spoiled mayonnaise may be the cause of the food poisoning.

In October 1981, Dr. Harold Jaffe, another young CDC epidemiologist, went to San Francisco to conduct a case-control study among homosexual men with and without Kaposi's sarcoma. Some of the men without Kaposi's were patients of private physicians; others had attended a public clinic for the treatment of sexually transmitted diseases such as gonorrhea and syphilis. One of the topics Dr. Jaffe asked about was sex. The answers were illuminating:

> The men with Kaposi's reported having an average of 61 different partners in the previous year; the public clinic patients and the men from private physicians said they had had about 25 different sexual partners in the past year. Both these numbers are much higher than the two to five sexual partners per year common among nonmonogamous [sexually active with more than one partner] heterosexuals. The ill men reported contacting a much higher percentage of their partners in "gay baths," public places where gay men can go for anonymous sex. The men with Kaposi's had met half of their partners in the baths; the clinic patients had made one-fourth of their sexual contacts in the baths; and the healthy private patients averaged only one anonymous partner per year.

Dr. Jaffe reported his results as follows:

> We have identified a syndrome associated with a lifestyle practiced by a subgroup of the homosexual population. The most important feature of this lifestyle appears to be having sex with a large number of anonymous partners.

In the second study, these results were verified by New York University epidemiologist Dr. Michael Marmor. About half of the AIDS

In the early days of the epidemic, some gay nightclubs were closed by the police because AIDS was thought to be a "gay" disease. In fact, AIDS is a worldwide health threat that can afflict anyone.

patients Dr. Marmor interviewed said they had been with more than 10 sexual partners in the last month. Only about 15 percent of the healthy homosexual men he talked to reported having this many.

This was not the first time an illness had been associated with the extremely active sex lives of some gay men. Several years earlier the same situation had been discovered for the infectious diseases hepatitis, syphilis, and gonorrhea. At that time CDC sociologist Dr. William Darrow wrote:

> Homosexual men have higher rates of sexually transmitted diseases than heterosexual men and women because gay men tend to have larger numbers of different sexual partners, more often engage in furtive [anonymous] sexual activities, and more frequently have anal intercourse.

The role of high sexual activity in spreading these diseases is easy to understand. The more sexual contacts, the more likely there will be exposure to someone who is infected. The same principle applies to catching the flu. If you go out in public more often during flu season when more people may sneeze and cough on you, you are more likely to be infected with flu virus.

Approximately 300,000 people marched in this parade in San Francisco in 1983 to alert the nation to the growing need for public cooperation in combating AIDS.

Although in retrospect it seems clear that all the evidence pointed to a new infectious agent as the cause of AIDS, this conclusion was not so obvious at the time. There were just too many variables. For example, their high rate of sexual contacts made gay men prone to many infections—herpes virus, CMV, hepatitis, gonorrhea, and intestinal parasites called amoebae. Did this high rate of infection itself have a deleterious effect on the immune system? Could the immune system ultimately be "stressed out" from constantly fighting off invaders?

This suggestion, called the *antigenic overload theory*, was discounted at the time by Dr. Gottlieb. He pointed out that many groups in history, and even now in Third World countries, have been subject to constant infections. "Yet no failure of the immune system of this dimension has been documented previously, which is a good argument for a new infectious agent as the cause of this new disease."

That still left puzzling questions: Why had this disease appeared at this time in history? If it was caused by a new infectious agent, where had the agent come from? The answers to these questions did not begin to come into focus until 1984, and they are not completely clear even now.

PUZZLING SYMPTOMS

Any theory of the new disease also had to account for a puzzling factor: the variety of symptoms seen in AIDS patients before they entered the final phase of complete susceptibility to opportunistic infections and cancers. Interviews with AIDS patients revealed many had been very sick for up to a year before they developed their first case of *pneumocystis* pneumonia or showed their first Kaposi's spot, both signs of AIDS.

One form of illness that preceded outright AIDS was a state called lymphadenopathy syndrome, or LAS, in which the patient had several swollen lymph nodes for three months or more. These swollen lymph nodes might be in the neck, in the throat, or under the armpits. Swollen lymph nodes are a sign that the immune system is fighting an infection. Did any patients with swollen lymph nodes get better, indicating a successful fight? Or was the struggle always futile? Several physicians recruited patients with LAS and examined them every few months to learn the answer.

A more serious condition was AIDS-related complex (ARC), a stage of the illness no longer considered separately. It had been defined in 1983 as the presence of two or more unexplained clinical symptoms of AIDS and at least two abnormal lab tests for the related signs. Patients with ARC might lose a large amount of weight, have frequent fevers, sweat a lot at night, feel very fatigued, and suffer untreatable diarrhea. It seemed that the presence of ARC signaled that outright AIDS was inevitable. But what phase of the AIDS disease process did ARC represent? The Centers for Disease Control never officially recognized ARC for its reporting purposes, but the term was useful in describing what appeared to be the onset of AIDS. Better terminology has followed from medical advances, however, and the symptoms of what was called ARC are now viewed as just another of the AIDS-related illnesses rather than as a distinct stage of the disease.

Throughout the early months of the epidemic, the spotlight was on homosexual men. In fact, for a time in 1981, the outbreak was called

GRID—Gay-Related Immune Deficiency. But by December 1981, when the first articles on the new syndrome appeared in the prestigious *New England Journal of Medicine*, a new group of victims had been found—intravenous heroin users. The destructive reach of AIDS was getting longer.

CHAPTER 3

THE EPIDEMIC EXPLODES

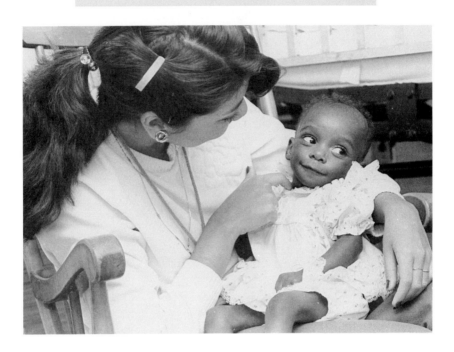

t is only a few miles from New York University Medical Center, the Sloan-Kettering Cancer Center, and the other hospitals on Manhattan's East Side where the first gay AIDS patients with Kaposi's sarcoma were diagnosed, to Montefiore Medical Center in the North Bronx. But in social terms the distance is light-years. Among the patients at Montefiore (though by no means all of them) are the poor black and Latino residents of the Bronx, as well as the IV drug users who come to the hospital for the only care available to them.

It was at Montefiore in autumn 1981 that Dr. Gerald Friedland saw his first cases of AIDS—men with *pneumocystis* pneumonia and ravaged immune systems. To Dr. Friedland, a specialist in infectious diseases who kept up with the medical literature, that sounded like the illness that had been cropping up in gay men in Los Angeles, San Francisco, and elsewhere in New York. But his patients were not gay: their wives and children were visiting them in

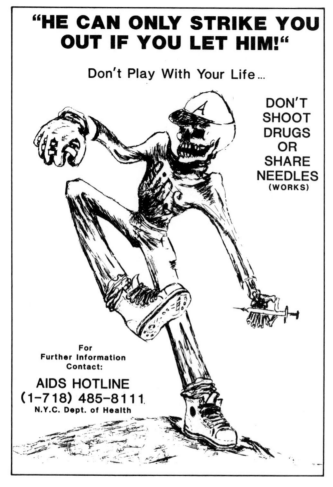

"HE CAN ONLY STRIKE YOU OUT IF YOU LET HIM!"

Don't Play With Your Life...

DON'T
SHOOT
DRUGS
OR
SHARE
NEEDLES
(WORKS)

For
Further Information
Contact:
AIDS HOTLINE
(1-718) 485-8111
N.Y.C. Dept. of Health

The practice among intravenous drug users of sharing needles has placed them in the highest danger category for contracting and spreading AIDS.

the hospital.

The initial association of the syndrome with gay men almost caused the doctors to miss the new connection—the men all injected heroin by needle. Even more important, they shared needles with other addicts.

INTRAVENOUS DRUG USERS

Heroin addicts have an illegal habit and are dedicated primarily to getting their next fix. Many do not stay in one place long enough to be studied. Most would rather use their money for drugs than for medical care, so they do not often enter the traditional medical system. Hence, relatively little is known about the medical condition of those who populate the drug culture.

Some impoverished intravenous drug abusers frequent the shadowy twilight world of South Bronx "shooting galleries," bombed-out, derelict buildings where heroin abusers can buy the magic elixir they crave and rent or share a needle to shoot it up with.

Sticking a needle into your vein after someone else has used it is an easy way to get any infectious diseases that the other person may have. It is like giving yourself a transfusion of infected blood. That is why IV drug users have a very high rate of hepatitis, a blood disease that is lethal if left untreated. That is also why they became the second group among whom AIDS rapidly spread. Within a year of the onset of the epidemic, almost 20 percent of AIDS patients were found to be IV drug users. By 1988, that figure had risen in cities like New York to between one-third and one-half of all AIDS cases.

Controlling the spread of AIDS among IV drug abusers is essential to stopping the AIDS epidemic. The gay men who make up about two-thirds of AIDS cases are, in general, sexually isolated from the larger heterosexual community of Americans, so they pose a much lesser threat of contagion to the public at large.

But most IV drug users are heterosexuals. Many female addicts resort to prostitution to support their habit. An infected prostitute can spread AIDS to any of her customers, and those men can spread it to any women or men they later have sex with. Former addicts can also transmit AIDS to any person they have a sexual relationship with, if they acquired the AIDS infection while they were using drugs.

By the end of 1981, the two main routes of AIDS transmission had been identified. The epidemiologists investigating the catastrophic epidemic grew more certain that AIDS was caused by an infectious agent. The pattern was so much like other sexually transmitted infections, such as hepatitis.

From these mysterious and frightening beginnings among gay men and IV drug users, AIDS was about to show its versatility by appearing in several new population groups. Indeed, epidemiologists were anticipating this development. If the new syndrome could be spread by sex between two men, they asked themselves, might it also be transmitted by sex between a man and a woman? And if it could be spread by blood on contaminated needles used by heroin addicts, could it also be spread by blood used for medical purposes, such as during surgery? The answers to both questions turned out to be affirmative.

Women are at high risk of getting AIDS if they have sexual intercourse with infected men or if they share needles with them.

WOMEN CAN GET AIDS TOO.

AIDS
YOU CAN GET AIDS BY HAVING SEXUAL INTERCOURSE WITH A PERSON WHO IS INFECTED WITH THE AIDS VIRUS OR BY SHARING NEEDLES WITH THAT PERSON.

PROTECT YOURSELF
• USE CONDOMS (RUBBERS)
• DON'T SHOOT UP–DON'T SHARE NEEDLES OR WORKS

CALL THE AIDS HOTLINE
1 (718) 485-8111
9 A.M. – 9 P.M. MON – SAT
STRICTLY CONFIDENTIAL

EVERYONE NEEDS TO KNOW MORE ABOUT AIDS.

OTHERS AT RISK

Between the end of 1981 and the end of 1982, several new groups were rapidly identified who were at greatly increased risk for contracting AIDS. They were as follows:

- Women who had sex with men who had the AIDS infection.
- Babies born to women infected with the AIDS virus.
- Hemophiliacs who injected blood products containing a clotting factor.
- Surgery patients who were transfused with contaminated blood.
- Newly arrived immigrants from Haiti and their sexual contacts.

In each instance, transmission was either through sexual contact or through receiving infected blood. It is essential to recognize that as each risk group was identified, it fit one of these patterns of transmission. There was no group of unexplained AIDS cases that could have been spread by casual contact, such as being sneezed on by a person with AIDS or eating food prepared by a person with AIDS. From May 1981 to the present, all evidence has confirmed that AIDS is spread only by intimate contact, not by the day-to-day, public encounters we all have in our business and social lives.

But with regard to the two ways that AIDS is transmitted, blood and sex, it is clear the illness does not select particular groups to afflict. It does not matter whether you are a man or a woman, or what type of lifestyle you practice. If you are injected or transfused with contagious blood or take into your body other contagious bodily fluids, such as vaginal secretions or semen, you run a high risk of getting AIDS.

Minute amounts of these fluids pose very little threat of transmitting the virus, and most nongenital fluids, such as saliva, are currently thought to pose no risk whatsoever of transmitting it. There is, however, a *theoretical* risk involved when any fluid is passed from an infected person, though the relative risk is extremely small. Research is still being done to prove these conjectures.

Early in the epidemic it became clear that men could transmit the infection to women. In several cases in which a man acquired AIDS through IV drug use, the woman with whom he was living and having regular sex also developed AIDS after a year or two.

It is not difficult for AIDS to be contracted through heterosexual activity. A group of doctors at Jackson Memorial Hospital in Miami studied the partners of a group of heterosexual AIDS patients. Over about two years, close to half of the partners became infected with the AIDS virus. Results of the Miami study also showed that over time the infection passes just as easily from women to men.

Among the IV-drug-using population further tragedy struck. Two doctors in the New York/New Jersey area started seeing infants with a syndrome very much like AIDS. They were Dr. Arye Rubenstein at Albert Einstein Hospital in the Bronx and Dr. Michael Oleske at St. Michael's Hospital in Newark. Adults at those hospitals included many women who had contracted AIDS through IV drug use or by having sex with a man who had gotten it that way. If one of those women became pregnant, the doctors realized, her baby had a high probability of developing AIDS in the first year after birth.

For many months other doctors were reluctant to believe infants were getting AIDS. The symptoms of the disease were not exactly the same in children as in adults. But, Drs. Rubenstein and Oleske argued, the immune system of an infant or child is still immature. The results of destroyed immunity in young children would be different. By spring 1983 they had proved their case. AIDS in newborns and young children was accepted as yet another grim side of this epidemic.

Between 1988 and 1995, the federal government's CDC conducted a program in 45 states to test newborns for AIDS. The testing was kept anonymous because 80 percent of the babies born to HIV-infected mothers never develop AIDS—even though they test positive at birth, because all newborns carry their mother's immune cells. Testing newborns helped the CDC track AIDS in young women.

The program was controversial for a number of reasons. On one side, legislators like Rep. Gary Ackerman (D-NY) asked for a requirement to tell mothers the results of the tests so they could seek treatment if the child was infected. On the other hand, AIDS activists argued Ackerman's suggestion was tantamount to mandatory AIDS testing for women, which they insisted would scare some women away from health care.

However, these same activists were stunned when the CDC suspended this survey. "This is one more misstep in a series of missteps," said Terry McGovern of the HIV Law Project in New York. "It was a political decision . . . The study has been really useful." In the early years, it provided the only evidence AIDS was becoming a danger to heterosexual women, McGovern explained.

Later the same year, CDC officials finalized guidelines calling for four million pregnant Americans to receive counseling, and urged voluntary AIDS tests. The guidelines were drafted when new research showed infected women can cut their chance of passing the disease to their baby by two-thirds if they take the drug AZT during early pregnancy. "We can save hundreds of babies' lives this way," CDC AIDS Chief Dr. James Curran told a congressional health subcommittee. "And every pediatrician will know every baby who is exposed."

By May 1995, the CDC was reporting AIDS had become the fourth-leading cause of death among women of childbearing age, and cases were increasing by about 8 percent among women. Some 7,000 HIV-infected women were giving birth each year and 2,000 of their babies were infected.

The following year, Congress once again considered mandatory AIDS testing for infants and passed a compromise bill in May 1996 that gave individual states the chance to cut the rate of AIDS transmission or to demonstrate voluntary prenatal testing before they would be federally required to conduct mandatory AIDS testing of infants. The bill, which passed 402-4, was named after an Indiana teenager who died after contracting AIDS from a blood-clotting product. It also authorized billions of dollars to state and local governments to care for AIDS patients and set a new formula to direct money to midsize cities and rural areas.

The bill also bars the government from providing grants to any organization or state unless the state requires a good-faith effort to notify current and former spouses of HIV-infected patients that they may have been exposed.

HEMOPHILIACS

Transmission of AIDS between IV drug addicts was assumed to occur via contaminated blood that remained on the needle after the person with AIDS had used it. It soon became apparent that AIDS could be spread by blood in other situations.

One of the first pieces of evidence for this idea was a report to the CDC in January 1982 from doctors in Miami. A 55-year-old hemophiliac man had died of *pneumocystis* pneumonia. At first the doctors thought the man's blood-clotting injections had transmitted *pneumocystis*. They soon realized that the injections had carried something far more pernicious—AIDS.

There are several diseases in which blood does not clot properly. Those born with these conditions lack one of the many elements in the blood that are essential to stop bleeding. Hemophilia A is an inherited clotting disorder that afflicts men almost exclusively. In a person with severe hemophilia A, internal bleeding or bleeding into joints can lead to serious complications, possibly even death. Even small cuts clot slowly. It was persons with severe hemophilia A who were at highest risk to get AIDS.

To control their bleeding tendency, hemophiliacs inject themselves with a concentrated preparation made from the blood of persons with normal clotting ability. This preparation, called *Factor VIII*, is credited with increasing the life expectancy of hemophiliacs in the last two decades from 35 to 55 years. Some hemophiliacs have a mild disorder and use Factor VIII only when they actually have a bleeding episode. But all hemophiliacs depend on it at some time.

Factor VIII, which was lifesaving for hemophiliacs, suddenly turned into an instrument of death. The preparation is made by pooling blood collected from 2,000 to 5,000 donors, then concentrating it, quick-drying it, and putting it in vials. Because so many people's blood was represented in each vial of Factor VIII, the possibility existed that at least one donor had AIDS or was harboring the AIDS organism—especially because drug users (until concerns were raised about infected donors) often sold their blood for cash. And because each hemophiliac uses 20, 30, or 40 vials of Factor VIII each year, there was a good chance that he would encounter a contaminated vial sooner or later.

This situation did not change until March 1985, when two steps were taken to make Factor VIII safer: manufacturers started testing all blood used to make Factor VIII for the presence of the AIDS organism; and they started heating all Factor VIII to kill any undetected AIDS agent.

AIDS FROM BLOOD TRANSFUSIONS

It was quickly realized that there was a much greater dimension to the problem of AIDS spread through blood. Every person who underwent surgery and received a replacement blood transfusion ran the risk of getting the disease. The risk was very small, only one or two chances in a million at the start. But as AIDS spread through the population, the number of infected units of donated blood increased, and the chance of getting an AIDS-infected transfusion during surgery increased.

News about the spread of AIDS through blood transfusions frightened many people and generated some misconceptions. Blood donations decreased because some people mistakenly believed that AIDS could be contracted while donating blood. That is not true. AIDS is passed by receiving contaminated blood through transfusion.

Many people demanded to have their own blood removed before surgery, stored, and reinfused into them during the operation if they needed it. This practice, called autologous transfusion, is feasible (except in the case of emergency surgery) and will protect the patient from getting AIDS through transfusion. hospitals and blood banks resisted at first, but now the practice is encouraged, and most hospitals are equipped for autologous transfusion.

Another practice, directed donation, is not necessarily safe. Directed donation means a patient's relatives and friends donate blood and direct that it be given to that patient. The problem: how can any patient know for certain that none of his friends or relatives harbor the AIDS infection?

Transfusion-related AIDS cases have remained relatively few. But these cases have been disproportionately frightening. Before there was a test to eliminate contaminated blood, no one had any control over whether he or she would receive a contaminated transfusion. And the choices for sick people were not appealing—have a necessary medical treatment and risk AIDS or allow your medical problem to continue.

By 1985, however, a way had been found to screen blood for the presence of the AIDS organism. This procedure eliminated over 90 percent of the risk of getting AIDS through transfusion. More sophisticated methods of testing have been developed since then. The risk of contracting AIDS through transfusion dropped from 1-in-2,500 in 1986 to 1-in-500,000 ten years later.

Along with increased safety, however, comes increased cost. Blood banks began charging hospitals ten times more than previously, to cover their costs. Testing regulations were tightly controlled, but with increasing competition some blood centers disregarded FDA safety regulations and their own internal standards to hold costs down. The FDA also investigated reports that employees of blood centers occasionally tampered with blood tests and falsified test results so potentially contaminated blood could be shipped without leaving a paper trail. In one case, both the FDA and Manhattan's district attorney launched criminal investigations of the New York Blood Center. Although very few units of AIDS-contaminated blood were actually used in hospital intrafusions, there were reports of infection with AIDS or other diseases, such as Hepatitis B.

THE ENIGMA OF THE HAITIANS

One more clearly defined group of AIDS victims exists—Haitian immigrants to the United States. The first Haitians with AIDS were seen in Miami at Jackson Memorial Hospital in 1980, soon after the 1979 influx of poor Haitian immigrants called "boat people." A number of the immigrants came to the hospital with wasting diseases. Some had brain infections; others died of uncontrollable tuberculosis. In a middle-class, native-born American these deaths would have been strange. But it was known that Haiti was impoverished and medical care was lacking. People still died there of diseases long conquered in the United States. So

Many of the Haitian "boat people" who came to the United States in 1979 were infected with AIDS.

at first, few were alarmed over the dreadfully sick Haitians in Florida.

But as the AIDS epidemic was publicized during 1981 and early 1982, it became obvious that the symptoms of some sick Haitians were very similar to those of AIDS patients. Dr. George Hensley of Jackson Memorial finally called the CDC after examining the brain tissue of a patient who had died of a brain infection with the tuberculosis bacterium. The appearance of the brain under the microscope was unlike anything he had ever seen in 22 years of examining postmortem tissues. The CDC sent an investigator, and recently arrived Haitians were added to the AIDS list.

For the most part, Hatian AIDS patients brought the disease with them, rather than catching it after they arrived. As the infected people die, and with no large new influx of Haitians, the number of cases of AIDS among Haitians in the United States is actually declining.

But the Haitian AIDS cases in the United States, though few in number, were critically important for another reason: they were the first indication that AIDS was not just an isolated American phenomenon. Their illness pointed back to the Caribbean island country of Haiti, implying that AIDS was also a native problem of that country. It quickly became obvious that AIDS was a worldwide problem of staggering dimensions.

THE GLOBAL EPIDEMIC

All the time that Dr. Hensley and the other Miami physicians had been puzzling over the desperately ill Haitian immigrants, rumors were leaking out of Haiti that the island had its own AIDS outbreak. When American epidemiologists became convinced that the sick Haitian immigrants in Miami had AIDS, Dr. Hensley decided to investigate the Haitian situation firsthand.

In June 1982 and again a month later, he went to Port-au-Prince, Haiti's capital, and pored through medical records at the main hospitals there. He became convinced that AIDS was a problem in Haiti, although the lack of thorough medical records made it difficult to determine just how great a problem it was. There were cases of death from CMV infection, *pneumocystis* pneumonia, Kaposi's sarcoma, the *candida* infection called thrush—the symptoms of AIDS patients in the United States.

While looking through the records, Dr. Hensley tried to answer a question many people had been asking: had AIDS come to the United

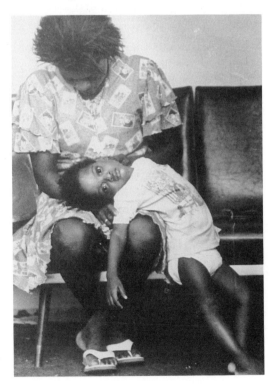

Most Haitian immigrants, such as this mother and child, were in poor health upon arriving in the United States. Scientists soon learned that heterosexuals, not homosexuals, were the chief carriers of AIDS in Haiti.

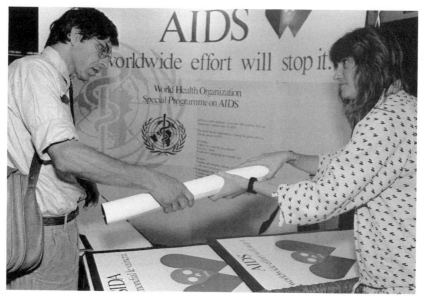

The global scope of the epidemic is staggering. Health organizations are gearing up to inform and educate all segments of the world population.

States from Haiti? The first cases appeared in the United States in the late 1970s. How far back could he trace AIDS cases in Haiti?

THE TRAIL GOES COLD

The earliest AIDS-like illness that Dr. Hensley could find in any Haitian hospital record occurred in October 1978. That was not significantly earlier than the epidemic had begun in the United States. "The upshot of the whole thing is that we found that AIDS had started at about the same time in Haiti as it did in the U.S.," Dr. Hensley concluded. "So it is no more likely that the disease was imported into this country from Haiti than vice versa."

Soon after Dr. Hensley's visit, the Haitian government closed its medical records to doctors from other countries. They were afraid of what might come out, afraid that their country would become known as the home of AIDS. In a desperately poor country that derived a large part of its income from tourism, that was a great threat.

Haiti's Minister of Health, Dr. Ary Bordes, accused the United States of using his country as a scapegoat. He blamed the outbreak of AIDS in

Haiti on American gays. According to Dr. Bordes, they infected the young Haitian men who practice homosexual prostitution as a source of income in a country with few jobs.

Unfortunately, this controversy obscured the answer to an important question: How was AIDS spread in Haiti? The Haitian government claimed to have proof it was by homosexual practices, but it would not release the data.

It was not until 1986 that a study by independent Haitian doctors settled this question. They found that some AIDS patients in Haiti practiced male prostitution. But up to 75 percent of the cases in that country, they concluded, were caused by heterosexual contact.

TRACKING THE EPIDEMIC

Haiti was the first country outside the United States in which AIDS was found to be spreading. Many larger countries soon followed. By late 1987, AIDS cases had been reported from 126 countries, mostly in Africa, Europe, and South America. By 1996, the epidemic had exploded. In its November *Morbidity and Mortality Weekly Report*, the CDC noted that the HIV pandemic had resulted in an estimated 27.9 million infections and 5.8 million deaths worldwide.

That same month, the United Nations and the World Health Organization (WHO) reported that HIV infection was appearing in previously unaffected communities in central and eastern Europe and Asia. Particularly hard hit, according to the report, were women and children. Of the 3.1 million new HIV infections recorded worldwide in 1996, 50 percent occurred in women, and 1,000 children were being infected every day.

Dr. Peter Piot, executive director of UNAIDS, the United Nations' AIDS program, said, "The HIV epidemic is far from over, and in fact it continues to strengthen its grip on the world's most vulnerable populations. Amidst all the optimism about new treatments, we must remember that 90 percent of people living with HIV/AIDS are in developing countries with little access to health care."

In one area of the Ukraine, for example, the percentage of IV drug users infected with the virus jumped from 1.7 percent in January 1995 to 56.5 percent in December 1995. "The only true hope for the entire world is prevention—education efforts, new forms of protection, and development of a vaccine," Dr. Piot said.

AIDS

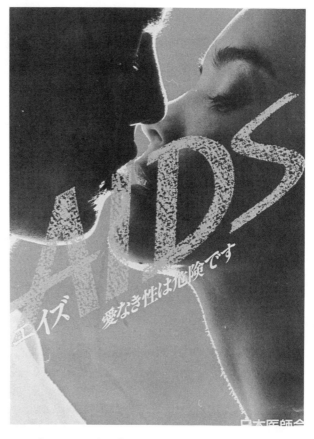

Right now, the forecast is most grim for Asian countries. While HIV-infection rates are dropping in Europe and the United States, health experts warn that HIV is mushrooming in Asia. About 800,000 people have been infected in Thailand, and that number is expected to rise to over a million by the year 2000. Up to one million people in Indonesia and 300,000 in Vietnam are expected to be infected by 2000.

Asians marked World AIDS Day on December 1, 1996, with calls to halt the spread of the epidemic. Thousands of people in Thailand distributed condoms at massage parlors and even gas stations, while in Manila, 500 members of HIV/AIDS Network Philippines released hundreds of red balloons labeled "World AIDS Day." Awareness groups in Tokyo marked the day by opening a 24-hour telephone-counseling service in eight languages and hot lines for Japanese women and homosexuals. Despite these events, experts believe a lack of education and cultural or religious taboos against open discussion of sex or the use

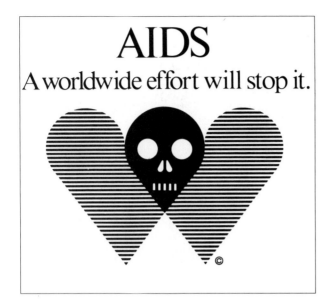

AIDS
A worldwide effort will stop it.

The AIDS logo of the World Health Organization, which is tracking the disease and attempting to prevent it from spreading further.

of condoms will ensure the killer disease will continue to run rampant in the region.

In India alone, the number of people infected with HIV could jump from 5 million in 1996 to between 20 and 50 million, according to the World Health Organization.

Part of the problem is apathy. "There has not been enough official attention given to AIDS," said I.G. Gilada, secretary-general of the Indian Health Organization. "People are suddenly waking up now that the situation looks like it's getting out of control."

Before the recent explosion of AIDS in Asian countries, the area with the largest number of AIDS cases was Africa. Several countries there were once European colonies, such as the Democratic Republic of the Congo (formerly called the Belgian Congo and Zaire) and Chad. It was Belgian and French doctors who saw the first African AIDS patients, well-to-do Africans who went to Europe for their medical treatment.

For many years African governments refused to talk about their AIDS problem, some even denying that it existed. Their motives were similar to the feelings of Haitian officials: they did not want their countries accused of being the source of AIDS. Mixed in with scientific evidence suggesting that AIDS originated in Africa, they felt, was racial prejudice against black people. At an international AIDS meeting in Brussels, Belgium, in November 1985, several black African doctors and scientists refused to present papers they had prepared about AIDS in their home countries.

A breakthrough of sorts came in November 1986 at a meeting of 37 African nations with WHO officials in Brazzaville, Congo. African government representatives admitted publicly that there was an AIDS problem on their continent and several solicited WHO's help and advice. In October 1987 Zambian president Kenneth Kaunda pleaded for help from WHO after his son died of AIDS. It is estimated that 20 percent of Zambia's adult urban population is infected with the AIDS virus. At that time, it was estimated that one out of every 1,000 adults in central Africa was infected with HIV—a figure 10 times higher than in the United States. What made this even more devastating was the grim fact that in many countries, the annual health budget amounted to less than $3 per person. There was no way these countries could even begin to cope with the problem alone.

In African countries, AIDS afflicts men and women equally because it is spread largely by heterosexual contact. There appears to be a higher level of sexual activity among African heterosexuals than in heterosexuals living in the United States, as well as a higher frequency of blood transfusion for such diseases as malaria. Both of these practices expedite the spread of AIDS. Men there also have a more frequent contact with female prostitutes than men in Western countries.

By May 1987 there were about 5,000 AIDS cases in Western Europe and perhaps 1 million persons infected with the AIDS virus. The highest percentage of the population infected was in Switzerland, particularly Zurich. France had the greatest total number of cases. On average, one child with the AIDS virus was born each day in France.

Germany, Italy, and Britain have had substantial numbers of AIDS cases as well. The British government became worried enough in the fall of 1986 to mount a massive public-education campaign. Leaflets about AIDS were mailed to every household. At the same time, public announcements were run on television and placed in newspapers.

In Europe, AIDS is spread mainly by homosexual activity. There is considerable spread by IV drug use as well, particularly in Italy and Spain. Many cases of AIDS in Europe stem from their former colonies, either from Europeans who contracted AIDS while working in an African country or from native Africans who emigrated to Europe, then found they had AIDS.

By 1996, the number of new AIDS cases relative to the total popula-

ESTIMATED TOTAL NUMBER OF AIDS CASES IN ADULTS AND CHILDREN FROM THE LATE 1970s UNTIL LATE 1995

ESTIMATED: 6,000,000 AIDS CASES

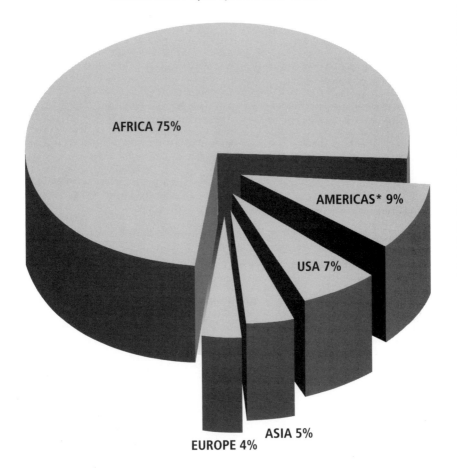

AFRICA 75%

AMERICAS* 9%

USA 7%

ASIA 5%

EUROPE 4%

Source: World Health Organization Global Program on AIDS   *Excluding USA

tion was leveling out, and in some cases declining, according to a report approved by the European Commission. As in the United States, AIDS in the nations composing the European Community (EC) occurred most frequently among gay men earlier in the epidemic, but in recent years the new diagnoses showed that HIV infections were much more likely to result from IV drug use. In those EC member nations where the association between AIDS and drug use is greatest—Spain, Italy, and Portugal—the number of new cases has continued to expand.

The EC invested $17.5 million in 134 international prevention and study projects during 1994–95 under the "Europe Against AIDS" action plan. The newly approved progress report on that plan included statistical findings from the European Center for the Epidemiological Monitoring of AIDS. Of the 22,383 new cases identified in 1996, 28 percent were infected through male-male contact while 43 percent were infected through intravenous drug use and 19 percent through heterosexual acts. Twenty percent of those infected were women. Continued efforts by the EC are part of its "Program for the Prevention of AIDS and Certain Other Communicable Diseases," adopted in 1996 and scheduled through the year 2000.

In South America, the country hardest hit by AIDS is Brazil. Both rich and poor are contracting the disease. By July 1987 Brazil was second only to the United States in reported AIDS cases in the Americas. But world health officials believe that there are actually many more AIDS cases in Brazil. Many cases go unreported because of the stigma attached to the diagnosis.

Homosexual transmission predominates in Brazil, as it does in the United States. It is thought the disease came to Brazil from the United States, where upper-class homosexual or bisexual Brazilian men have been known to seek sexual partners. The first cases probably appeared in Brazil in 1982, and the numbers have been increasing ever since.

The Brazilian government has mounted a large public-health campaign to combat AIDS transmission. Officials are especially busy during the annual Carnival festival, when planeloads of tourists come from other countries—including many homosexuals from the United States—for the revelry. Half a million leaflets about AIDS were distributed, with instructions on how to avoid getting it.

CHAPTER 4

IDENTIFYING
THE VIRUS

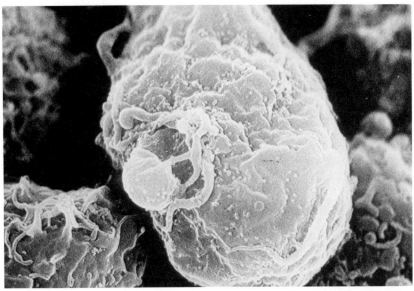

AIDS virus attacking cell (magnified 150,000x)

By spring 1983, the AIDS epidemic had been recognized for two years. Its modes of transmission, by blood and sexual contact, as well as other features of the epidemic, suggested to most scientists that the basic cause of AIDS was an infectious agent. The search for infectious organisms in AIDS patients had turned up many familiar disease-causing bugs. But none of them could explain the new syndrome.

In particular, no known infectious agent was capable of producing the specific destruction of the immune system that AIDS causes. Underlying all the symptoms of AIDS is one primary defect: loss of a pivotal type of white blood cell called the *T4 helper lymphocyte*. The role of T4 lymphocytes is to help other types of immune cells become active and do their job. Without the T4 helper cells, the immune system virtually shuts down. And in some AIDS patients there was an almost complete loss of T4 helper cells.

Scientists familiar with the AIDS epidemic had to face an unpleasant truth: they were dealing with an unknown agent, possibly something completely new to science. This would not be like isolating the infectious organism that caused Legionnaires' disease. That task had taken only six months because the Legionnaires' organism was closely related to a family of known bacteria. The methods for growing and identifying it were familiar.

To address the possibilities, the National Institutes of Health (NIH), a federal research institution, invited many top scientists to a conference in spring 1983. The purpose of this conference was to generate new ideas about where the causative agent of AIDS might be found. More specifically, they wanted to discuss viruses.

VIRUSES AND BACTERIA

Viruses are the most minute form of life. Some people might not even call viruses living organisms. They are many times smaller than bacteria, the other major cause of human infectious disease. Whereas bacteria are independent, able to grow and reproduce outside the cells of the organism they infect, viruses are parasites. In order to make more of their kind, viruses must enter the cells of the creature they infect and take over the cellular machinery. They subvert its productive power by making more of their own kind. The cell dies, but the virus thrives.

Once the virus that causes AIDS was isolated, tests were developed to detect its presence in blood.

The virus is an intracellular parasite because its structure, unlike that of a bacterium, is too rudimentary to sustain itself—it must live within another cell (Bacteria are internally complex, containing all the equipment necessary for life). Viruses contain only the genetic material necessary to propagate themselves and a tightly wrapped protective coat of proteins.

These differences lead to a crucial medical distinction between bacteria and viruses. Twentieth-century medical science has developed many antibiotic drugs, such as penicillin, to combat bacterial infections. But viruses are more difficult to kill. Because they reproduce inside our own cells, it is difficult to find drugs to stop the virus from reproducing without harming the host cell. Progress against diseases caused by viruses—such as polio, smallpox, measles, and mumps—has come through use of vaccines, which prevent infection. Almost all American children get vaccinated for such viruses at an early age.

When the NIH meeting convened, most scientists believed a virus caused AIDS. There were many reasons. Quoted in *People* magazine in February 1983, Dr. James Curran, the head of the CDC's AIDS unit, explained two—latency and persistence.

Latency means that the infection stays in a person's body for a while before it causes clinical illness. Because viruses can lie dormant inside cells, they can have long latency periods. The latency period for AIDS—the time between exposure to the infection and the first symptoms—may be as long as eight years, but it is usually three to five years. In children the latency period is much shorter, and in women it may be shorter than in men. *Persistence* refers to how long the infectious agent remains after it starts the disease. With AIDS it is most likely that the agent stays for the person's remaining lifetime. Despite treatment of each opportunistic infection, the immune system remains impaired. As fast as new immune cells are made they are destroyed.

THE NEXT HURDLES IN THE RACE

Isolating HIV allowed several aspects of the epidemic to be explained more fully. Why was such a spectrum of illnesses associated with AIDS, ranging from the flulike illness that occurred when a person was first infected to full-blown AIDS? The answer is that many viruses can cause a range of disorders of varying severity. When polio was rampant before a vaccine was developed, it caused several levels of illness. Some people were infected and got a temporary flulike illness. Others were paralyzed but recovered. Still others had to live in an iron lung, and some died.

Once the AIDS agent was identified, the source of the epidemic could be further investigated. Viruses similar to HIV have now been isolated in various types of African monkeys and apes. These primate viruses are distantly related to HIV.

One tentative conclusion is that a viral ancestor of HIV evolved in Africa millions of years ago and affected monkeys. Gradually it changed to the form of HIV we see today. But this still does not explain why the virus suddenly started causing human disease in the last quarter of the 20th century.

The most important long-term benefit of the isolation of HIV was that it allowed scientists to begin working to develop a vaccine against AIDS. That process is expected to take several years. The most immediate practical impact of the isolation of HIV was that a test could be devised to detect the presence of the virus in a person's body long before he or she showed the symptoms. The test could be used to identify blood containing the AIDS virus, making the nation's blood supply safe again; it could also give an estimate of how widespread HIV infection was. When those results came in, they were quite ominous.

PROFILE: ISOLATING THE VIRUS

Dr. Luc Montagnier of France (left) and Dr. Robert Gallo of the United States were the first to identify the Human Immunodeficiency Virus (HIV), which causes AIDS.

Scientific advances can involve heated competition and personality disputes, just as in any other field. The race to isolate the AIDS virus ended with such a dispute, which momentarily overshadowed the importance of the accomplishment itself.

Dr. Robert Gallo, working in his research lab at the National Cancer Institute in Bethesda, Maryland, had already discovered a human cancer retrovirus, a form of virus so named because its cells reproduce themselves in a way opposite to that of common viruses. He found some evidence to suggest that this retrovirus was the cause of AIDS. He and his colleagues published several of their reports in the May 1983 issue of the authoritative journal *Science*.

But in the same issue there appeared a single report from a group of French scientists headed by Dr. Luc Montagnier, of the renowned Institut Pasteur in Paris. This research team, too, had isolated a retrovirus that they thought was the cause of AIDS. It was similar to the one found by Dr. Gallo's group.

Dr. Gallo named the retrovirus that he found HTLV, for human T-cell lymphotropic virus. Dr. Montagnier's virus was isolated from a patient with the pre-AIDS syndrome of swollen lymph nodes. He named it LAV, for lymphadenopathy-associated virus.

The two viruses were thought at the time to be similar, but not identical. Only one could be the true cause of AIDS. The question was, which one? In the balance were prestige, profits, and awards.

The conflict seemed to be over in spring 1984. With reputations at stake—both individual and scientific—each team published new research in *Science*. The American scientists' results were announced at a dramatic press conference presided over by the secretary of the U.S. Department of Health and Human Services, Margaret Heckler.

Secretary Heckler proclaimed that U.S. science had "hit the bull's eye," because it was Dr. Gallo who had found the agent responsible for AIDS. The guilty agent was not HTLV, but a new virus that Gallo's team had just isolated and named HTLV-III (the third variant of HTLV). Though the French scientists had been building their case for LAV over the past year at meetings and in papers, their work was ignored at the press conference.

Could AIDS be caused by two different viruses? No. Further comparison of LAV and HTLV-III showed them to be virtually identical, and charges of scientific thievery arose. The French and American governments began a lawsuit, each contending that their teams had found the virus first. The scientists themselves, to their credit, took little part in the squabble.

The dispute over which scientific team had first isolated the virus extended to its name. Should it be called HTLV-III or LAV? An international commission reached a compromise by giving the virus a different name altogether—human immunodeficiency virus, or HIV. That is the name by which the virus is now generally known.

The lawsuit was settled in 1986, with an agreement to split the recognition and possible rewards from the virus's discovery. The awarding of the prizes has also been neutral. The Lasker Award for 1986 went to both Dr. Gallo and Dr. Montagnier.

In 1995, after 30 years of government service, Dr. Gallo left the U.S. National Cancer Institute to start the Institute of Human Virology as part of the University of Maryland. The new Institute focuses on AIDS but also researches other human viral diseases and cancer.

Dr. Montagnier, who now is the head of the Department of AIDS and Retroviruses at the Institut Pasteur, continues his research on the role of antioxidant nutrients as a key part in slowing the progression of HIV infection to the AIDS state. He also is experimenting with the use of antibiotics, such as tetracycline, to delay the onset of AIDS in HIV-infected people.

CHAPTER 5

HELPING
THE VICTIMS

hen the first cases of AIDS transmission through donated blood appeared in 1982, public-health officials looked for a way to protect the blood supply. Various tests were proposed, and though none would be completely effective because the cause of AIDS was not yet known, they would help. Some blood-bank physicians objected to using the tests on the grounds that they would cost tens of millions of dollars.

With the discovery of the AIDS virus, HIV, in spring 1984, one of the major benefits touted by government officials was that it made possible the development of a blood test that would reliably prevent HIV-contaminated blood from getting into the blood supply. It was a sign of the impact that the growing epidemic was making on the American consciousness that no one contended any longer that using such a test would be too expensive. Today, all blood banks routinely test for AIDS.

THE BLOOD TEST

In concept the AIDS blood test is simple. It is based on the body's immune reaction to infection. When a foreign organism, such as HIV virus, first enters the body, the immune system gears up to produce specially designed substances called *antibodies*. Antibodies are carefully shaped so that they attach only to parts of the foreign organism that they are intended to protect against. This attachment is the first step in the body's campaign to rid itself of the invader.

In HIV infection, antibodies and other components of the immune reaction are apparently not strong enough to kill the invading viruses. Nonetheless, the immune system continues to churn out antibodies to the virus. Even when the virus has almost totally destroyed the immune system, some antibody-producing cells are still active.

The bottom line is that any person who has been infected with HIV has forever after in his or her blood antibodies to attack different parts of the virus. Therefore, to find out whether a person has ever had HIV infection, it is only necessary to take a sample of blood and search for these antibodies. The discovery of HIV and its growth in laboratory cultures made it possible to perform this search.

The anti-HIV antibodies in the patient's blood are swimming in a sea inhabited by many other substances. The test's objective is to fish out one of the anti-HIV antibodies and measure it. What is needed is the proper bait, and the bait comes from the virus itself.

Because antibodies are made against parts of the virus, the testing method is to prepare a large amount of virus, purify one of the viral components, and add it to the blood being tested. If an antiviral antibody is in the blood, it will snap shut around the viral material and not let go. The next step is simple: reel it back in and identify it.

Any blood bank can now purchase ready-made kits that will detect those units of donated blood that come from a person who has been infected with HIV, even if that person looks completely healthy. Infected units of blood are either thrown away or used in research.

The reason for not transfusing blood containing anti-HIV antibodies is not the presence of the antibodies themselves. It has to do with the feature of viral persistence mentioned earlier. Scientists believe once a person is infected with HIV, that person will always harbor the virus. This theory has been tested by attempting to isolate the virus from samples of blood that tested positive in the HIV-antibody test. The virus was found to be present in virtually all the samples tested.

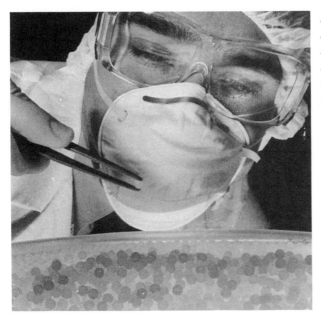

Blood testing procedures are now highly advanced. This technician is examining biochemically treated beads for a reaction that would indicate the presence of HIV.

CONSEQUENCES OF THE TEST

The AIDS blood test became available in the middle of 1985. It was immediately put into use all over the country, in every facility that collected blood for human use, to test for the presence of HIV. For the most part this removed one of the most threatening and unpredictable sources of AIDS infection.

But the widespread acceptance of the AIDS blood test has other, more disturbing consequences. Some of these include:

- Will there be adequate counseling to explain the meaning of a positive test result, and to provide psychological support to ease the shock of a positive result?
- Will it be possible to keep confidential the names of persons who test positive?
- Should insurance companies be allowed to demand AIDS testing as a condition before providing insurance?
- If a person is rejected for military service because of a positive AIDS test, what does that person put on later job applications?
- Is it fair for corporations or employers to require an AIDS

test as a condition of employment?

- Is large-scale testing of the entire population justified to decrease the spread of AIDS?

To young people today, these issues are vital. Just as tomorrow's adults will have to know how to live with the presence of AIDS, they will also have to know how to make their way in a society where the AIDS test is a fact of life.

TESTING AND LOOPHOLES

How good is the HIV-antibody test? As tests go, it is very accurate. Out of every one million blood samples, perhaps only four are erroneously declared free from HIV.

There are some minor loopholes in the test's ability to detect blood from an infected donor. In most persons, between one and six months must pass after infection for enough antibodies to be generated for the test to register positive. So people who have only recently been infected may have a false-negative result. A small number of people may not test positive for up to a year after infection.

A greater drawback to the HIV-antibody test is that it falsely indicates the presence of HIV antibodies in some samples that do not actually contain them, the "false-positive" result. For this reason every positive reading from an HIV-antibody test is further checked with a more specific but more time-consuming test called a *Western blot*. In this test the blood components are separated in an electrical field, and any anti-HIV antibody present is directly visualized.

HOME HIV TEST KITS

In the summer of 1996, the Food and Drug Administration approved the first two home HIV test kits—Confide, marketed by Johnson and Johnson, and The Express Kit, marketed by Home Access Health Corporation.

The kits enable a person to take a blood sample in the privacy of his or her own home and then send it to a laboratory for analysis. Both tests require just a dot of blood for analysis. After the sample is sent, the individual calls a toll-free number and gives their special identification code, to ensure anonymity. Experienced counselors operate the phone lines to answer questions and provide support and referrals on request.

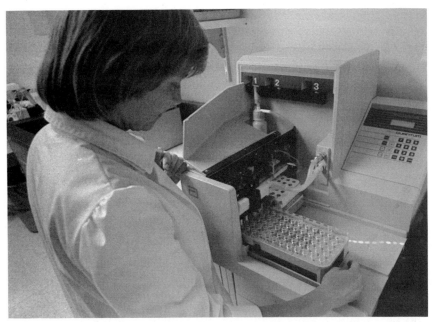

If the AIDS virus is present in blood, natural antibodies will have formed. Tests for AIDS are designed to detect these antibodies.

Most experts believe the potential benefits of self-test kits outweigh the drawbacks, which include questions of test contamination, psychological impact, consent issues, and other ethical concerns related to cost of and access to treatment. Some people felt testing should remain the responsibility of physicians and hospitals, while others argued the public already had proved it could responsibly use similar home tests for pregnancy and high cholesterol.

SALIVA TESTS

In January 1997, the *Journal of the American Medical Association* unveiled a highly accurate alternative to blood-sample testing for HIV—the saliva test. Researchers had known for more than a decade that the saliva of infected individuals contains low levels of HIV antibodies. The problem was that the enzymes in saliva also destroy the antibodies. In the new test, called OraSure, a cotton fiber pad is placed between the gum and cheek for two minutes, then placed into a preservative solution that prevents degradation of the sample.

According to the AMA report, the test is 99.9 percent accurate in sensitivity—detecting both those with HIV infection and determining those who are not HIV-positive.

Experts felt the availability of a simple, noninvasive, reliable alternative to blood-sample testing would increase access to HIV testing, and therefore counseling and therapeutic care. Other advantages of the test include increased safety for health care workers—who would not use a needle or lancet to obtain a sample, as they do when taking blood—and an alternative for people who are squeamish about giving blood to get tested.

Currently, the saliva test is designed to be used in a doctor's office, with the oral sample shipped to laboratories for testing. Research is being conducted to develop a home-use version of the saliva test similar to the home blood test kits already on the market.

COUNSELING

One critical service must be provided by every institution doing the HIV blood test, and that is counseling. When the first positive blood test result is communicated to the patient, a trained counselor must explain that nothing is certain until another test can confirm that result. The counselor must communicate the real possibility that the result is a false positive.

Later, for those patients whose antibody-positive status is confirmed, the counselor must explain this result, too. It does not mean that the person has AIDS, but it does mean that the person has been infected with HIV and must assume he or she could infect others. An HIV-positive person has a responsibility to tell all lovers or his or her spouse about the condition, and must take precautions against transmitting the virus when having sex, as the infection probably will never go away.

The counselor also must take the first steps toward helping the antibody-positive person absorb the shock of learning of his or her infection. The patient probably felt fine upon coming in for the test and didn't expect to hear a result that could be a death sentence.

THE OFFICIAL U.S. DEFINITION OF AIDS

A person who is found to be HIV-positive may ask another question: does that mean I have AIDS? In the early years of the epidemic, this was

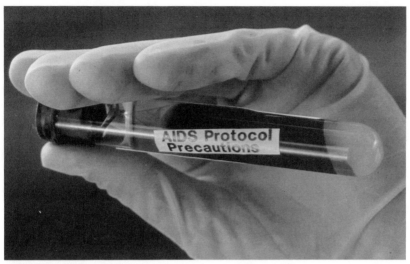

Medical personnel have to take extra precautions to avoid exposure to the virus while working on infected patients or with laboratory samples.

a tough question to answer because studies had not followed the course of the disease in HIV-infected people for a long enough period to know if HIV inevitably led to the onset of AIDS.

In 1993, to help people understand the relationship between HIV and AIDS, the CDC presented the *Official U.S. Government Definition of AIDS*. The government needed to classify the different stages of HIV infection in order to clearly define who was eligible to receive government assistance. Under the government's classification system, an HIV-infected individual can fall into three categories. There are two factors which determine the category: T-cell count and history of disease symptoms.

The T-cell (officially called CD4+T-lymphocyte) is the vulnerable immune-system cell the HIV virus attacks, then uses as a breeding ground. Eventually, the T-cell is killed by the virus. As a person's T-cell count decreases, the risk of severe disease, or "opportunistic illness," increases. The three official levels of T-cell counts are:

Level 1: a T-cell count greater than 500 cells/ml
Level 2: a T-cell count between 200-499 cells/ml
Level 3: a T-cell count less than 200 cells/ml

These categories are based on the lowest T-cell count registered by a person. For example, someone who once tested at 180 but later received a boost in T-cells from a new protease inhibitor would still be considered at Level 3.

To determine the three official government classifications, symptoms are also a factor. For example, a patient is in AIDS Category 1 if he or she is asymptomatic (no symptoms) and has a Level 1 T-cell count. An AIDS Category 2 patient has a Level 2 T-cell count and at least one of the early-stage illnesses listed on Page 24-25 (such as thrush, shingles, or diarrhea and fever lasting two weeks or longer), but has not developed a later-stage disease, such as pneumonia or Kaposi's sarcoma. In Category 3—full-blown AIDS—the T-cell count has dropped below 200 and the patient has developed a later-stage disease.

TESTING THE PUBLIC: OTHER PROBLEMS

Some proposed uses of the HIV-antibody test for nonmedical, non-research purposes raise serious social and ethical questions. For instance, insurance companies, eager to avoid paying the huge medical bills incurred by AIDS patients, have started using the HIV test to exclude infected persons from coverage.

There has been strong objection to this action. One argument runs: why not test everyone's cholesterol and exclude those with a high value, since they are at risk for a heart attack? In August 1987, New York State prohibited insurance companies from denying coverage to persons who test positive for HIV. California has done the same.

Some employers are considering demanding an HIV-antibody test as a condition of employment. Whether this will stand up in court as a valid requirement is still an open question. It is not clear what purpose the test would serve. As long as they remain healthy, infected persons can continue to do their jobs, and they are not infectious in typical office contacts.

In June 1987 President Reagan issued a directive that all immigrants and federal prisoners be tested. He also recommended mandatory testing of all persons applying for a marriage license.

In Georgia, judges can order convicted prostitutes to be tested. Some persons want doctors and nurses tested as well: a 1987 Gallup poll found that 80 percent of Americans believe that health-care workers should be tested for HIV and that patients should be informed if they are about to be treated by an HIV-positive doctor or nurse.

Some doctors, for their part, would like to know whether their patients are infected. Surgeons, in particular, point out that they have

In 1987, President Ronald Reagan recommended widespread AIDS testing; however, many people feel mandatory testing violates constitutional rights.

prolonged and extensive exposure to a patient's blood during an operation. A few hospitals have begun routine HIV testing of all patients admitted for surgery.

There are situations when not divulging the HIV-positive status of an individual puts another individual at direct risk for unknowingly contracting the disease. For example, a man who tests HIV-positive may withhold the information from his wife because he doesn't want her to know about his extramarital relationships. If no one tells her, she does not have the choice of protecting herself against infection.

But who should have the power to decide who gets told and when? Some countries have dealt with this ethical dilemma by passing confidentiality laws. In May 1995, for example, Norway passed its Communicable Diseases Control Act, which makes it compulsory for a physician to warn a third party if it is obvious that an HIV-positive patient is placing others at risk for infection. Under the law, however, before the physician breaks medical confidentiality, he or she must try repeatedly to gain the consent of the patient involved. Obviously, skilled counseling is needed to make sure this does not jeopardize the patient's willingness to cooperate with a positive plan of treatment.

In the United States, in the earlier stages of the epidemic, the confidentiality of HIV-related information about a patient was protected by law. Any doctor who breached the obligation of confidentiality faced the possibility of a lawsuit for economic, bodily, or psychological harm resulting from the wrongful disclosure. He or she also faced criminal liability for knowingly disclosing the results of an AIDS blood test in a manner that identified the person to whom the test results apply.

But by the 1990s, confidentiality was no longer an absolute duty. The patient's identity was protected, even though the doctor was required to report new AIDS cases to the Department of Health Services. But a physician who confirmed that a patient was HIV-positive was now permitted—ethically and legally—to disclose that information to the patient's sexual partner.

Prior to such third-party notification, however, the physician was required by law to discuss the test results with the patient and to offer appropriate educational and psychological counseling. The doctor also had to attempt to obtain the patient's voluntary consent for notification of contacts. If the patient continued to refuse, the physician was required to advise the patient the notifications would be made even without the patient's consent.

Normally, a doctor was not legally required to notify third parties, but was permitted to do so. Only in situations where the patient exhibited manic-depressive or reckless tendencies did the physician have a legal duty to warn others, particularly if there was a possibility the infected patient might purposely try to expose others by unsafe sexual encounters. If a patient's sexual partner was not notified of the risk of HIV infection in this context and became infected as a result, the doctor could have been sued for failing to provide a warning.

In late 1996, some legislators tried to pass a controversial bill through Congress called the HIV Prevention Act. In an effort to prevent more Americans from contracting HIV and to improve the quality of life of those who are infected, the bill mandated the reporting of all HIV cases and imposed criminal sanctions on people who knowingly transmitted the virus through sex or drug needles. It emphasized partner notification as a way of identifying possible carriers of the virus. However, the bill was tabled for further discussion.

CHAPTER 6

THE FIGHT
AGAINST AIDS

There were more advances in HIV treatment during 1996 than in any other year of the epidemic. New drug combinations that include the antiviral compounds called *protease inhibitors* were reversing AIDS symptoms and lowering virus levels dramatically for many patients. By early 1997, statistics were beginning to emerge that suggested a dramatic drop in the death rate in areas where the new treatment was being offered. Both New York and San Francisco reported AIDS-related deaths dropped by at least half between the beginning and end of 1996. A study in British Columbia, Canada, found that in the last three months of 1996, the AIDS death rate for the province was one-third what it had been two-and-a-half years earlier.

Experts agreed that improved treatment was almost certainly the main reason for the decline in deaths and that over time the figures might become even more dramatic. It will take years before meaningful data can be obtained on the long-range effects of the new treatments.

Although there are new treatments for HIV that have helped slow the onset of AIDS, many people in the United States and around the world cannot afford this expensive medical care.

OPTIMISM DOES NOT APPLY GLOBALLY

But despite the encouraging decrease in deaths during 1996, AIDS experts have been very guarded in their optimism. For one thing, it was quickly discovered the anti-HIV drug "cocktails" did not work at all for 10 to 30 percent of the patients. Even more important, the great majority of people around the world with HIV, including many in the United States, do not have access to expensive medical care from experienced physicians or the costly drugs that make up this new treatment.

That is not true only for Third World countries. Even in the United Kingdom, it was reported that persons with HIV were less likely to receive modern combination treatments due to funding problems. In the United States, quality of care varies greatly by social class and by region.

There also is a third factor that causes experts to hesitate in their optimism. Even with access to the best care, no one knows if the improvements in 1996 will be permanent. Will deaths continue to decrease, or will 1996 be an exception?

Even if these new treatment breakthroughs lead to an AIDS cure and a vaccine, the battle is far from over. No treatment, vaccine, or cure is going to be effective until it is available to every at-risk person on Earth.

THE FOCUS SHIFTS TO THE THIRD WORLD

The theme of the 11th International Conference on AIDS held in Vancouver, British Columbia, in July 1996, was "One World, One Hope." Its aim was to signify the spirit of a global community fighting together to control the HIV pandemic. For the first time, there was a feeling that the recent therapeutic advances, and some of the prevention successes, were indeed having some effect. However, the grim statistics made it equally clear that the burden of the HIV pandemic was shifting almost entirely to Third World countries—countries that could not afford any of these new treatment advances without international help.

Some of the sobering statistics provided at the meeting were from the newly-formed UNAIDS, the joint United Nations program on HIV and AIDS. This group estimated that 21.8 million adults and children were living with HIV or AIDS by the end of 1996—94 percent (20.4 million) of them in the developing world. Close to 19 million people with HIV or AIDS—86 percent of the world total—live in sub-Saharan Africa or Southeast Asia.

In 1995 alone, 2.7 million new adult HIV infections occurred, an average of 7,500 per day. Of these, about 1 million (an average of nearly 3,000 per day) occurred in Southeast Asia, and 1.4 million (nearly 4,000 per day) occurred in sub-Saharan Africa. The industrialized world, by contrast, accounted for 55,000 new HIV infections in 1995, or only 2 percent of the global total. Of the 1.6 million children with AIDS in the world, the majority, 1.4 million (88 percent), live in sub-Saharan Africa. To date, an estimated six million people have died of AIDS.

As the meeting progressed, it became clear that in the world of AIDS there really are two worlds. One is composed of industrialized nations where the epidemic has stabilized and where enormous advances in therapy have resulted in increased survival for those infected with HIV. The second is comprised of developing countries where the epidemic is still a runaway train. At an estimated annual cost of $15,000 per person for therapeutic intervention, there is little chance that residents of a small African village will be among the fortunate recipients of these emerging treatment successes.

This woman contracted AIDS from her husband, a former intravenous drug user. She died a few months later.

EIGHT DISTINCT STRAINS OF HIV EMERGE

At the beginning of 1997, Dr. Thomas C. Quinn, a federal researcher who combined estimates from the World Health Organization with reports from national health agencies worldwide, and a Harvard team headed by Dr. Jonathan Mann, former AIDS chief for WHO, reported epidemic control measures, including the widespread distribution of free condoms in Thailand's brothels and to the general public in Zaire, were curbing the epidemic's spread in some urban centers, but that in many other areas the disease continued to spread unabated. And in America, although the impact of AIDS remained heaviest among gay men or IV drug users, heterosexual transmission of the virus was increasing rapidly and cases among women, teenagers, and young adults also increased.

What was particularly puzzling and horrifying to AIDS control specialists, according to Quinn's report, was that eight distinct varieties of HIV have emerged separately on different continents—a problem that will pose difficulties in developing vaccines and antiviral therapies.

CARING FOR THE STRICKEN

In the face of an overstressed medical system, volunteer programs have sprung up in both New York and San Francisco to help AIDS patients while they are out of the hospital. In San Francisco the gay community provides support and home-care assistance for AIDS patients. In New York City in 1983, the Gay Men's Health Crisis organization set up a similar program of meals, home services, and visits.

Caring for AIDS patients in the terminal stages is made especially difficult by HIV infection of the brain. This leads to neurological problems with movement and walking, as well as to dementia, a gradual loss of mental function. One nurse who has worked with AIDS patients compares HIV dementia to "literally losing your mind an inch at a time."

One answer to the difficulties of caring for severely ill AIDS patients is the establishment of outpatient and hospice care. By 1984 the Shanti Project in San Francisco had set up residences where AIDS patients could care for themselves and each other outside the hospital.

The first hospice in New York City was established by the Nobel Peace Prize–winning nun Mother Teresa, who was distressed by the

Former Surgeon General C. Everett Koop (center) tours an AIDS hospice in San Francisco. Koop was essential in promoting AIDS education during the early days of the epidemic.

Mother Teresa, who received the Nobel Peace Prize for her work with the poor in India, helped establish the first AIDS hospice in New York City.

plight of these patients. It was a natural response from a person who had established shelters for the poor of Calcutta, India.

The State of New York started a network of hospices in early 1986, the purpose of which is to provide not heroic medical measures but compassion and caring. Responding to the patients' distress at dying is a main feature of these hospices. "They are afraid of being left alone and abandoned," one nurse said. Enough of these beds had been established by mid-1987 to care for half of the city's AIDS patients. Around the country, many churches and private groups have set up care facilities and systems for local AIDS patients.

By the mid-1990s, however, the number of hospices in the United States had declined substantially. One reason for the decline was that families of AIDS patients became more willing to provide care themselves. Another was that treatment breakthroughs were keeping AIDS victims symptom-free and alive much longer, so fewer people needed hospice care.

CHAPTER 7

PUBLIC RESPONSE TO THE DISEASE

A IDS has not only caused upheaval in the medical world and in the lives of its victims; it has also precipitated conflict and change in almost every aspect of American life, both public and private. It seems that everyone who works on AIDS in any capacity has become part of the controversy, for they are sometimes accused of incompetence or bad intentions. In some people's minds, association with AIDS is as bad as the disease itself.

Many of the accusations have been ludicrous, such as the 1986 Soviet propaganda campaign to blame AIDS on U.S. germ-warfare tests, and a British scientist's assertion that AIDS is a secret Soviet germ-warfare weapon. Other charges have had to be taken more seriously, even though they were proven wrong. For instance, the CDC has persistently been accused of ignoring the possibility that AIDS is spread by a virus that infects pigs. This rumor was started by a scientist who thought that the symptoms of human AIDS patients closely resembled those of pigs infected with chronic African swine fever, a disease found in Africa and Haiti. Considerable scientific resources have had to be expended to disprove this idea.

Two scientists in Miami claimed that AIDS is spread by mosquitoes. They accused government scientists of conspiring to cover up the mosquito link to AIDS. The Miami scientists chose to ignore the fact that mosquitoes are common in many U.S. cities and African countries where there is very little AIDS. Experiments showed that a mosquito could take in HIV if it bit a person infected with the virus. But there is no evidence that the virus can survive and reproduce in the mosquito's body or that the insect can transmit the infection to people it later bites.

Normal legal and social relations have been radically altered by the fear of AIDS. In the mid-1980s, precautions against AIDS became widespread. These included hospitals supplying nurses who regularly gave injections with latex gloves, boxing referees wearing rubber gloves

Policemen wear latex gloves as a precaution while arresting demonstrators during an AIDS rally. The protesters were calling for more government action and research funds to fight the disease. The gloves were not necessary because AIDS cannot be spread by casual contact.

in the ring, and firemen and policemen wearing protective clothing in situations when they might come into contact with AIDS patients. Emergency Medical Service technicians, afraid of getting AIDS while handling injured AIDS patients, started to wear surgical suits, gloves, and masks while on duty. They also began using mouth protectors for giving mouth-to-mouth resuscitation.

In the arena of criminal law, there have been several unusual cases. In one, a prostitute bit a policeman. The judge had to decide whether he should try to compel her to be tested for HIV infection. A soldier infected with HIV was accused of aggravated assault for having sex with fellow soldiers. A military court ruled that his HIV test was not admissible as evidence. That ruling was overturned on appeal.

THE STIGMA OF AIDS

A few physicians have violated the accepted principles by falsifying death certificates of persons who died of AIDS. There have been some famous cover-ups, and many among less prominent persons, too. "I have a tendency not to put AIDS on the death certificate," said one doctor. "If the wrong person sees it, it could be a problem for the family."

The stigma of AIDS was demonstrated perhaps most dramatically in several cases in which young boys who tested positive for HIV were excluded from school. This happened in 1987 in a well-known case involving a young boy, Ryan White, in Kokomo, Indiana, and in the case of a Florida family whose three boys were infected. All these boys were hemophiliacs and had been infected through the blood-product injections they took to control their bleeding.

In the Florida case, a judge ordered the school to accept the children, saying exclusion was not justified by current medical knowledge. After that ruling, someone burned down the family's house, and the family felt compelled to leave the town. These situations show the outrage directed at a disease like AIDS, which is usually spread by means considered immoral by many people—homosexual sex and IV drug use. Disapproval is combined with fear of the lethal ailment.

AN "IRRATIONAL MINORITY"

In a poll published in *Newsweek* magazine in August 1985, only 25 percent of the people questioned said they would try to have a child

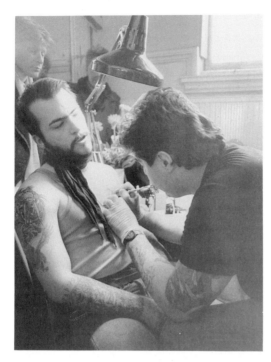

This tattoo artist is wearing gloves, illustrating the concern that AIDS can be spread by minute amounts of infected blood.

with AIDS removed from school or keep their own children home. But two years later a vocal and frightened minority dominated the situation in the Florida school case.

An even sadder situation is the refusal of a few physicians to treat AIDS patients. Most other physicians have condemned this type of behavior. Former Surgeon General C. Everett Koop called doctors who refuse to treat AIDS patients a "fearful and irrational minority" and accused them of "unprofessional conduct."

In the *Journal of the American Medical Association* of October 8, 1987, Dr. Edmund D. Pellegrino wrote, "The physician is no more free to flee from danger in performance of his or her duties than the fireman, the policeman, or the soldier." To their credit, most health-care professionals have devoted themselves unstintingly to caring for patients with this difficult disease.

At first, fear of AIDS led to proposals for coercive measures against HIV-infected persons. In 1986 a proposal was put on the ballot in California to test all citizens and to quarantine those who test positive. The measure was defeated, but the idea has been proposed in Texas and

A prostitute imprisoned for practicing her trade after she had tested positive for HIV.

other places as well. There even was a suggestion to tattoo all persons who had tested positive for HIV.

UNEXPECTED HEROES GENERATE SYMPATHY AND AWARENESS

But many Americans began to change their attitudes toward AIDS when someone they knew became infected—not necessarily someone they knew personally. For some, the change began in 1985 when film star Rock Hudson became one of the first of many celebrities to die of the disease. Although Hudson probably acquired AIDS through homosexual contact—a possibility that shocked many people—his death saddened the country and brought the reality of the disease closer to home for many Americans.

Another AIDS victim who touched many hearts was Ryan White, who died of AIDS in April 1990. One of the best-known early victims of

Ryan White, a hemophiliac, contracted AIDS through a blood-product injection. After he was barred from school, his fight to attend the public school attracted wide media attention and generated much controversy. Here he listens to classroom discussion over the telephone.

AIDS, the Indiana teenager had contracted the disease several years earlier through a contaminated blood product used to treat his hemophilia. The public became familiar with Ryan's case when his fight to attend public school attracted wide media attention and generated much controversy.

The next year, 1991, a young Florida woman named Kimberly Bergalis drew national attention when she made an impassioned plea before Congress for mandatory AIDS testing of all health-care workers, shortly before her death of AIDS. She had contracted the disease from her dentist.

In November of the same year, sports star Earvin "Magic" Johnson, a three-time National Basketball Association Most Valuable Player, stunned the world with his announcement that he had tested positive for HIV and was retiring from pro basketball on the advice of his doctors. He was not only the first major professional athlete to leave sports because of AIDS, he was also the first major public figure to attribute contracting the disease to heterosexual behavior. At his press conference, Johnson urged young people to abstain from sex outside of marriage or to practice safe sex.

In April 1992, another sports figure stunned with world with his announcement of AIDS—former tennis great Arthur Ashe. Because his achievements went beyond the tennis court, his announcement had an impact on many people. Widely respected and outspoken on racial issues, Ashe had gained fame as a political activist and social commentator. He believed he had contracted the disease from a blood transfusion during a surgical procedure in 1983. Ashe died within a year of his public announcement.

In 1994, 22-year-old Cuban-American MTV star Pedro Zamora died of AIDS. Before his death, Zamora made an educational video to be distributed to junior high and high schools. In it, he told his story to help other young people become aware of the risks of HIV infection. In addition, the Pedro Zamora HIV Clinic was founded in his name as part of the Los Angeles Gay and Lesbian Community Services Center. The clinic uses young people to spread medical help and advice because it feels there is a greater chance these volunteers will get through to teens, a group with one of the fastest growing rates of HIV infection.

THE ENTERTAINMENT INDUSTRY RESPONDS

By 1987, the entertainment media was becoming sensitive to the impact of AIDS on American society. Some movie producers became more restrained in their depiction of sexual activity. Sexual promiscuity was even eliminated from a James Bond movie produced in 1987 in deference to the cautious "new morality." Producers also began making movies that sympathetically portrayed characters living—and dying—with AIDS.

One of the first was *Parting Glances* in 1986. In it, two longtime gay roommates whose friend is dying of AIDS spend their final 24 hours together before one leaves for New York on a job transfer. This was starring actor Bill Sherwood's only movie; he died of AIDS in 1990.

Perhaps the best-known film about AIDS is the 1993 movie *Philadelphia*. In it, a gay lawyer stricken with AIDS seeks assistance from a homophobic personal injury attorney when a prestigious Philadelphia

When movie actor Rock Hudson died of AIDS in 1985, public recognition of the disease's impact began to grow.

law firm fires him for incompetence. Critics called it a sensitive and heartfelt look at the effect of AIDS on family, friends, and the people who interact with an AIDS victim.

In theater, Larry Kramer's 1985 powerful production *The Normal Heart* is considered the first major play written about AIDS, followed by William Hoffman's *As Is* and Harvey Fierstein's *Safe Sex.* AIDS continues to be a powerful theme in the theater.

AIDS has become a theme in other artistic media as well, both for artists who themselves have become infected with the disease and for those who choose to vividly depict its effects on humanity. It has become a way for victims to express their courage and faith as well as their anger and fear.

New York's Museum of Modern Art observed an AIDS Awareness

Day on December 2, 1996, to commemorate the tragic impact of the AIDS epidemic and to offer hope and support for those suffering from AIDS or HIV. The day-long program included readings, a dance performance, and a discussion about new therapies for AIDS, as well as AIDS-related art by the Toronto art collective General Idea. Similar exhibitions and performances have been scheduled in cities throughout the country and in many parts of the world.

Artists such as Elton John have used music to show their concern and support. John started an AIDS foundation in November 1992. The singer/songwriter donates a percentage of the profits of his own recordings to AIDS research. In 1993, the foundation's first fund-raiser, the First Annual Academy Awards Viewing Party, raised more than $125,000, and there have been numerous successful fundraising events since.

GROWING AIDS ACTIVISM

By no means have all media stars—or Americans in general for that matter—favored public support of AIDS research and care for victims. Some celebrities and politicians gained notoriety for opposing AIDS support and often have become targets for demonstrating AIDS activist groups. At Ronald Reagan's 85th birthday party in 1996, for example, 300 demonstrators banged drums, blew whistles, and created a disturbance to draw attention to what they called "genocidal Republican AIDS policy." House Leader Newt Gingrich, California governor Pete Wilson, former chairman of the Joint Chiefs of Staff Colin Powell, and other Republican leaders also have been targeted for their opposition to government funding of AIDS programs.

People with AIDS began forming activist groups in 1987, demanding more attention from the government, scientists, and the pharmaceutical industry. In 1992, both major political conventions featured moving speeches from women with HIV—Elizabeth Glaser at the Democratic convention and Mary Fisher at the Republican convention.

According to a monthly publication called *AIDS Treatment News*, by January 1997 there were well over 10,000 national and local AIDS organizations in the United States alone, including the AIDS Coalition to Unleash Power (ACT UP), the National AIDS Treatment Advocacy, National Association of People with AIDS (NAPWA), and the AIDS Coalition. In 1992, the AIDS in Prison Project established the first

AIDS/HIV Clearinghouse and Free Bilingual Hotline for prisoners and former prisoners with AIDS. There also is a 24-hour-a-day National AIDS Hotline (800-342-AIDS) that refers people to these and other groups and provides other referral information.

AIDS advocacy groups have had a certain amount of success in bringing the urgency of AIDS issues to the attention of national legislatures. In a budget compromise reached in late 1996 between the White House and Congress, an additional $100 million in funding for AIDS services was added. What made a funding increase possible,

After Los Angeles Lakers star Magic Johnson announced that he was HIV positive, he started promoting AIDS education and urged young people to abstain from sexual contact or practice safe sex.

according to a poll conducted by the *Washington Post*, was the continuing concern of the public. Their poll showed that AIDS ranked second among public concerns, tied with crime and slightly behind education, despite the relative silence of politicians about AIDS.

AIDS MEMORIALS

Another example of the change in public attitudes toward the disease by the mid-1990s is AIDS memorials. By this time, the lives of hundreds of thousands of Americans had been touched by AIDS in some way. But now, instead of feeling shame and a need to conceal the fact that a loved one died of AIDS, many people wanted to make sure their tragedies would never be forgotten. In addition to the AIDS Quilt project discussed in Chapter 1, people all over the United States were urging legislators to provide funding for the creation of AIDS memorials. San Francisco has one of the largest and most impressive of these monuments—the AIDS Memorial Grove, a 15-acre wooded basin located in San Francisco's Golden Gate Park. In 1996, legislation was introduced proposing that the memorial be made a national monument.

CHANGED ATTITUDES TOWARD SEX AND EDUCATION

Fifteen to twenty years ago, condoms and homosexuality were the subjects of adult-only sex manuals, not family newspapers and TV dramas. That changed when the Centers for Disease Control and Prevention reported the first stages of a horrible epidemic—a wave of death spread by sex, blood, and shared drug needles. Social observers started calling this the "age of AIDS." One of the epidemic's greatest areas of impact probably has been on how Americans talk and think about sex.

One thing that has changed dramatically is the amount of public discussion of homosexuality. Gay men and lesbians "came out of the closet in record numbers" to join the AIDS fight, says Lorri Jean, executive director of the Los Angeles Gay and Lesbian Community Services Center. For many Americans, that meant accepting homosexuals as sons or daughters, friends, and caretakers.

Another change has been in sex education in America's schools. By

1996, 36 states were requiring or recommending sex education in public schools, up from only three in 1986. In spite of AIDS, the percentage of sexually active teenagers increased during the 1980s. Thanks to increased education, studies show sexually active teens, singles, and gay men are much more likely to use condoms today than 15 years ago.

A 1996 nationwide study sponsored by the Menlo Park-based Kaiser Family Foundation showed that AIDS education can increase knowledge and understanding of the disease among grade-school

ELIZABETH TAYLOR–LEADING AIDS ACTIVIST

I n February 1997, ABC aired "Happy Birthday Elizabeth—A Celebration of Life," a special star-studded tribute honoring the world's leading AIDS activist, Hollywood legend Elizabeth Taylor. The two-hour black-tie gala featured rare footage of

Elizabeth Taylor became one of the most outspoken AIDS activists after the death of her friend Rock Hudson. She has raised millions of dollars for AIDS treatment and research, and since 1992 her Elizabeth Taylor AIDS Foundation (ETAF) has funded organizations nationwide that provide services to men, women, and children affected by HIV or AIDS, as well as organizations conducting research to develop AIDS treatments and a cure.

children without increasing their fear. It also showed that two out of three Americans favor the distribution of clean needles to drug addicts to slow the spread of AIDS. A number of Americans were beginning to favor once-taboo AIDS prevention measures such as education for preteens, television advertising of condoms, and needle exchanges.

Americans remain split, however, on the issue of condom distribution in high schools. Forty-nine percent of those polled said students should receive only information in schools, while 46 percent

Taylor's life and career and appearances by such stars as Michael Jackson, Carol Burnett, John Travolta, Magic Johnson, and Rosie O'Donnell. One of the largest televised AIDS fundraisers ever, all the proceeds were donated to the Elizabeth Taylor AIDS Foundation (ETAF).

The ETAF, founded in 1992, has funded organizations nationwide that provide services to men, women, and children affected by HIV/AIDS, and supported organizations conducting research to develop AIDS treatments and a cure. Through ETAF, Taylor has also promoted AIDS education and prevention.

Taylor has been the largest single contributor to the American Foundation for AIDS Research's work on needle exchange, which supported the most comprehensive study ever on clean needle exchange. This landmark 1996 study was conducted by leading researchers at Beth Israel Medical Center and New York University Medical Center. Among other findings, it documented a two-thirds decrease in new HIV infections among injection drug users enrolled at five community-based needle exchange programs in New York City.

Taylor had many problems organizing her first AIDS benefit in Los Angeles in 1984 because no one wanted to publicly acknowledge the disease. That was before the death of her friend, fellow screen star Rock Hudson. "I have never known rejection like that before in my life," she said. "Then Rock became sick and that really hit the town and people did start to get involved. I had no idea then I would be taking the first step on such a long and heartbreaking road."

said schools should make condoms available to teenagers.

A growing body of scientific evidence supports the view that needle exchange programs—which allow injection drug users to swap a used hypodermic needle for a clean one—can reduce the spread of HIV infection without increasing drug abuse. But needle exchange programs are a very hot issue that many politicians either veto or avoid altogether because they don't want to appear "soft" on drugs. By the mid-1990s, nearly 70 needle exchange programs were operating nationwide, about half in direct violation of the law.

Christian and Jewish religious educators have published their own guidelines for developing AIDS educational programs in the 1990s. The programs address the spiritual and theological issues of AIDS, as well as the medical issues, by citing religious texts applicable to the AIDS epidemic. Minority groups also have addressed AIDS education. In May 1989, the Southwest Regional Hispanic AIDS Conference discussed problems of delivering AIDS education to the Latino community using culturally sensitive materials, and providing a network for Hispanic AIDS education and service agencies.

SYMBOLIC RED RIBBONS

A simple red loop of ribbon has become a powerful and instantly recognizable symbol of AIDS support. Visual AIDS, a nonprofit coalition of New York artists and art professionals, developed the concept in 1991, believing a simple red ribbon was a way to show support for those struggling against AIDS.

The ribbons became popular after they were first worn at the 1991 Tony awards; after that, it became commonplace to see celebrities wearing them at other award ceremonies, and the symbol quickly caught on. In New York, people began wearing them on the street, and in Orlando, Florida, a local AIDS organization distributed 600 at the NBA All-Star game. In England, 75,000 heavy metal music fans showed up at a rock concert wearing the ribbons.

Frank Moore of Visual AIDS explained that the color red was chosen for the ribbons because of "the connection to blood and the idea of passion—not only anger but love, like a Valentine."

CHAPTER 8

ENCOURAGING TREATMENT BREAKTHROUGHS

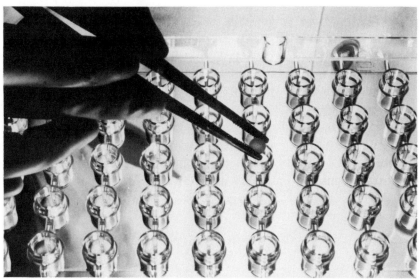

Testing blood for HIV

From the beginning, one of the most horrifying features of AIDS has been the relentless progression of the illness once HIV infection occurs. Until late 1996, there was little help available to halt, or even slow, that progression. Drugs were available, and new ones were being developed, to combat individual infections such as *pneumocystis* pneumonia, *candida*, toxoplasmosis, and Kaposi's sarcoma, but in patients without a strong immune system, these drugs were not very effective.

Before 1997, no one had ever recovered from AIDS once he or she was diagnosed. A large proportion of patients died within the first year after diagnosis and between 80 and 90 percent were dead within three years.

With the discovery in 1984 that AIDS is caused by HIV, the search for drugs to combat the powerful virus began.

EARLY ANTI-AIDS DRUGS

HIV is a member of a family of viruses called *retroviruses*. Scientists had been studying these viruses for several decades in tissue cultures and in laboratory animals such as rats, mice, and chickens—animals for which retroviruses are deadly. In particular, one that infects domestic cats is considered a major problem.

For a long time, no retroviruses were known that caused disease in human beings. In fact, scientists searched for many years to find a retrovirus that causes cancer in humans. When Dr. Robert Gallo of the National Cancer Institute did find a cancer-causing human retrovirus in 1980, it was a major feat.

But the retrovirus isolated by Dr. Gallo, HTLV, was the only known retrovirus that caused disease in humans, and even HTLV caused relatively few cases of cancer. So the search for drugs against retroviruses was not very active before HIV was identified as the cause of AIDS.

The first compounds to be tested on HIV as possible anti-AIDS drugs were chemicals that were known to prevent reproduction of other retro-viruses in the test tube. Several of these substances worked against HIV as well. Then came the difficult part—testing the active materials in humans infected with HIV to see whether they were active in the body and whether they caused undesirable side effects.

The first promising drug, called HPA-23, was tested by Dr. Luc Montagnier and his colleagues at the Institut Pasteur in Paris. A very hopeful early sign was the disappearance of the virus from the blood of a hemophiliac boy with AIDS. The boy even went back to school for a time. But eventually the virus reappeared. In addition, HPA-23 damaged the body's white blood cells.

In the United States early hope was raised by a drug already used against parasitic infections, called suramin. Again, the benefit was too small, the poisonous effect too great.

Several false leads were announced, one about the immunity-altering substance cyclosporine, and another about ribavirin, a compound used to combat a virus that causes breathing problems in infants. Both proved ineffective in humans with HIV infection.

The National Cancer Institute started a program in 1984 to interest pharmaceutical companies in testing any drugs they thought might be effective against HIV. The Institute would perform the initial laboratory testing, then help the company with clinical testing. Time and cost

Protestors demonstrate in 1986 against delays in the release of experimental drugs to treat AIDS. AZT was the first clinically useful anti-AIDS drug.

would be cut greatly by the Institute's assistance.

Out of this partnership came the first clinically useful anti-AIDS drug, which was called AZT, short for azidothymidine (its name has since been changed to zidovudine). AZT interfered in the backward step by which the retrovirus turned its RNA genetic material into DNA genetic material, which is necessary for the virus to take advantage of the cell's synthetic ability.

Initial tests with AZT were done in very ill AIDS patients. The study started in February 1986. By September it was clear that patients taking AZT were living longer and feeling healthier. The trial was judged definitive when investigators saw that patients not getting AZT were dying at a much faster rate than those getting the drug: Only one patient getting AZT died, compared to 16 deaths in the control group.

On March 21, 1987, the Food and Drug Administration approved AZT for clinical use. The approval process had taken just 18 months, a relatively speedy approval. AZT (marketed under the name Retrovir) was initially approved for certain very sick AIDS patients: those with *pneumocystis* pneumonia and those with other severe debilities of the syndrome's advanced stages, in which most of the immune cells had been killed. These patients taken together comprised more than half of all surviving AIDS cases.

Public officials emphasized that AZT was not a cure. But all AIDS patients wanted it anyway; it was all they had. Unfortunately, the drug is extremely expensive: a year's supply can cost as much as $10,000.

It has now been found that AZT, too, has serious side effects. Its chief drawback is that it can cause severe anemia, requiring blood transfusions. About half of AIDS patients cannot tolerate AZT.

An anti-HIV medicine can help AIDS patients, but it is not enough. Keeping the virus in check is the first step. In addition, some way must be found to restore the immune cells already killed by the virus. One early attempt was to transplant bone marrow from one twin without AIDS to a twin who had AIDS. (Bone marrow is a source of immune cells.) This is a standard medical procedure in some patients with leukemia.

PROTEASE INHIBITORS AND TRIPLE-DRUG THERAPIES

In January 1997, Dr. Harold Jaffe of the Centers for Disease Control and Prevention announced a stunning statistic: in the previous year, 1996, AIDS deaths dropped by 30 percent in New York, the U.S. city hardest hit by the epidemic. The next month, the Centers for Disease Control reported the number of AIDS deaths dropped significantly nationwide for the first time since the epidemic began in 1981. AIDS deaths fell 13 percent in the first six months of 1996, the CDC said.

At the same time, the CDC reported the growth rate of new AIDS infections slowed from five percent in 1993–94 to two percent from 1994–95.

"This is one of the first bright spots we have seen in this epidemic," said Christopher Portelli, executive director of the National Lesbian and Gay Health Association in Washington.

Part of the reason, of course, was the dramatic improvement in the survival rate since the introduction of protease inhibitors, a new class of drugs that revolutionized AIDS treatment. But the AIDS death rates began to improve even before the advent of protease inhibitors, so other factors, such as access to treatment, also played a significant role.

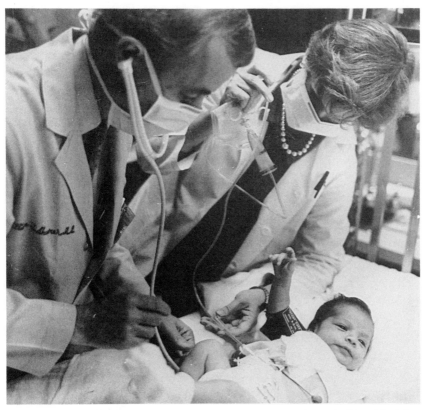

This baby is about to receive a bone marrow transplant in an effort to build up his deficient immune system. The operation is painful and expensive and is not feasible for most AIDS patients.

The HIV virus has been a formidable adversary. After infection, it spreads to the bloodstream, lymph nodes, brain, and even the body's chromosomes. But in 1996, 15 years after the first reported cases of AIDS, researchers developed a treatment that prolonged the lives of AIDS patients and offered hope for a cure. In 1996, the Food and Drug Administration approved five new drugs that, when taken in different combinations with AZT, appeared to put the disease into temporary remission.

About the same time, other researchers isolated a gene that appeared to protect some people from HIV infection, even after repeated exposure. This generated a good deal of excitement and hope for new genetic therapies and perhaps even a vaccine.

The arrival of new combination drug therapies rapidly transformed the AIDS epidemic in the United States, prolonging the lives of many AIDS patients and keeping them healthy enough to stay out of the hospital. Evidence also suggested that triple drug therapy, although extremely expensive, lowered the cost of treating many HIV-infected people by keeping them healthy.

At the Fourth Conference on Retroviruses and Opportunistic Infections in January 1997, researchers released studies that documented how patients in very advanced stages of AIDS benefited dramatically from the new drug "cocktails." People treated within months of being infected experienced a sharp, long-lasting reduction in levels of the virus in their blood and in tissue elsewhere in their body. Especially surprising to those attending the conference was the research from New York City's Department of Health showing the first significant decrease in AIDS-related deaths since records started to be kept in 1983.

Martin Hirsch, an AIDS research physician at Harvard Medical School, produced the first data suggesting that people infected with HIV for a long period also can benefit from the new drug combinations. In a study that followed 320 long-infected patients for six months, about 65 percent (55 of 85) of those who took a three-drug combination had the virus levels in their blood fall below the point where it was detectable by the most sensitive tests available. Researchers also reported that 18 of 21 patients on the same triple-drug combination but less further along in the disease had undetectable virus levels for more than 68 weeks, the longest anyone has reported a sustained success for the combination therapy.

In another much-anticipated presentation, Martin Markowitz from the Aaron Diamond AIDS Center, New York, updated the center's controversial experiment to eradicate the virus by treating patients with the cocktail therapies within 90 days of infection. Eighteen of 24 patients who have stayed on the therapy had no detectable levels of virus in their blood, some of whom had been treated for as long as 16 months.

DR. DAVID HO CREDITED WITH BREAKTHROUGH

In December 1996, *Time Magazine* pronounced Dr. David Ho of the Aaron Diamond AIDS Research Center in New York City "Man of the

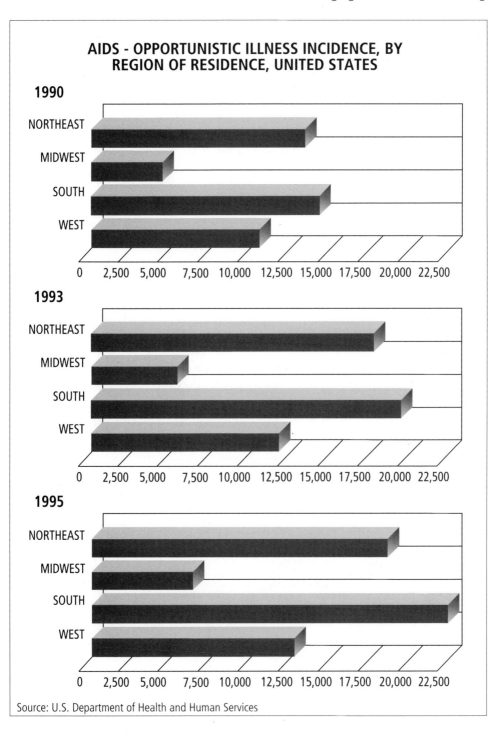

AIDS - OPPORTUNISTIC ILLNESS INCIDENCE, BY REGION OF RESIDENCE, UNITED STATES

Source: U.S. Department of Health and Human Services

Year" for research that led to important 1996 treatment breakthroughs. He was the first scientist to be named Man of the Year since 1960.

Starting in 1990, Dr. Ho and other researchers began focusing on the first stages of HIV infection—the period when an infected person seems in good health. They hoped to learn how the immune system fights the virus during this period, reasoning that with this knowledge, a way to help the body win its battle against the virus could be found. What Dr. Ho found out surprised him—and changed the way scientists think about HIV.

Until recently, researchers believed that after the HIV virus initially entered the body, it settled inside a few of the immune system's T-cells and remained dormant for the next seven to ten years. Then, something triggered the virus to suddenly seek out and destroy all the other healthy T-cells. In the process, it systematically destroyed the immune system by reproducing hundreds of thousands of copies of itself. Once the immune system was crippled, the body became vulnerable to all sorts of opportunistic infections.

What Dr. Ho and his research team discovered is that there is no initial incubation phase of the infection, as was previously believed. Instead, the invading virus and the defending immune system wage an all-out battle right from the moment of infection. Every day, the virus produces a billion copies of itself to attack the T-cells. And every day the infected immune system retaliated by producing a billion new immune cells to stop the virus from gaining ground.

The other amazing discovery Dr. Ho made was that the main battle-field for the virus and immune system was not the circulatory system as everyone had previously thought, but the lymph nodes, where day after day, year after year, the immune system successfully holds its own against the virus—until it finally exhausts its immunological reserves and the virus destroys the remaining T-cells and spreads to the brain.

Dr. Ho believed if treatment could be started early enough in the infection process to enhance the immune system's fighting power, the virus could not only be kept in remission, but perhaps even destroyed. The way to do it, he believed, was to combine several different antiviral drugs.

PROTEASE INHIBITORS

This was an exciting theory, but until 1995 there were not enough

Dr. David Ho developed a treatment involving several drugs called protease inhibitors. The combination treatment has been very effective in nearly eliminating the level of HIV in the blood of infected patients. For his work, Dr. Ho was named "Man of the Year" by Time Magazine *in 1996.*

different kinds of drugs available to test his approach. In December of that year, however, the FDA approved a new medication called saquinavir. One of the new so-called protease inhibitors, the new drug attacks the virus at an earlier stage than previous drugs.

Protease is an enzyme essential for the HIV virus to replicate itself. Protease inhibitors are molecular compounds specifically designed to inhibit, and thus interfere with, the replication process. Five peptide-based protease inhibitors were developed in the United States in 1996: saquinavir, A-80987, ABT-538, L735/524, and KNI-272/NCI.

Dr. Ho combined the new protease inhibitor saquinavir, the old standby AZT, and another new drug similar to AZT called 3TC, and in early 1996, began testing this "cocktail" on patients in advanced stages of the AIDS disease. Some of the patients didn't respond at all, possibly because they had become resistant to AZT or couldn't tolerate the powerful drugs, but in a number of cases the new therapy seemed to have forced the disease into total remission.

When it became obvious the cocktail was prolonging the lives of patients in later stages of the disease by months and maybe even years, Ho and his colleagues began trying it out on a dozen men still in the earliest stages of infection. A year later, these men showed no trace of HIV in either their blood or their lymph nodes, although the infection could remain in the brain.

NEW TREATMENTS LOWER COST

In President Clinton's strategy report for fighting AIDS in 1997, he estimated the cost of medical care for a person infected with HIV averaged $119,000. The good news: despite their relatively high price tags, new combination drug therapies could significantly lower the overall treatment costs for many patients. Two studies showed the treatments, which combine new protease inhibitors with older AIDS drugs, reduce the use of hospitals and other expensive services. The cost reduction is more than enough to make up for the expense of the drugs, which can easily cost $12,000 a year per patient.

The findings came at a crucial time. State AIDS drug-assistance programs, which receive federal funding to help uninsured, low-income patients buy medicine, were struggling to keep pace with the cost of the new treatments. This information gives AIDS activists a potent weapon in their effort to win increased state and federal funding for the new drugs.

Studies showed that in some areas between 1994 and 1996, the average number of days spent in hospitals each month by patients fell 57 percent, while the average number of days spent in hospices fell 65 percent. Need for home-care services also plummeted.

At the same time, the use of protease inhibitors more than doubled total medication costs from 1994 to 1996, and that cost quadrupled for patients in the most advanced stages of the disease.

THE DOWNSIDE OF TRIPLE-DRUG THERAPY

Although this breakthrough has already prolonged thousands of lives and may possibly lead to a cure, many HIV-infected people in the United States and Europe still have not benefited, either because side effects force them to quit therapy, the drugs' high costs put therapy out of their reach, or because the virus inside them has developed resistance to some of the drugs.

In addition, the optimism the combination drug treatment has

Dr. Jonathan Mann of the World Health Organization, which shoulders much of the AIDS global research and education efforts.

produced in Europe and North America isn't shared by the developing world, where 90 percent of new HIV infections are occurring and antiviral therapy of any sort is unaffordable.

"We are winning a small battle in a war that is being lost," said John W. Mellors, the head of the AIDS programs at the University of Pittsburgh Medical Center. "There is optimism for the individual in some places, but I don't have great optimism for controlling HIV anywhere."

AIDS BEGINS TO FIGHT BACK

In September 1997, doctors reported that AIDS was tougher than they had feared. The triple-drug therapy, which reduced levels of HIV in infected patients to almost zero, started to fail after about 18 months in about half the patients treated in some studies.

At an infectious disease conference sponsored by the American Society of Microbiology, Dr. Steven Deeks gave an update on a study of 136 HIV-infected people who started the drug cocktail therapy in

Although there have been treatment break-throughs in the past few years, there is still no vaccine for AIDS. Education about the disease and how to avoid contracting it remains important. At colleges such as Dartmouth College in New Hampshire, free "safe sex" kits are given to all students to help stop the spread of AIDS.

March 1996, when the first powerful protease inhibitors were developed. Most of the patients responded dramatically at first, with levels of the virus dropping so low they could not be found on standard tests. Since then, however, the virus has returned to detectable levels in 53 percent of the patients. Deeks said other large AIDS clinics were experiencing similar setbacks.

Unfortunately, no one knows what this means yet.

"There is a whole mixture of explanations" for the failures, Dr. Ho said after the report. He said that for people who had relatively low virus levels when the started taking the drugs and had not used other AIDS medicines, failure almost always meant they did not take their pills on schedule. Even missing a few doses of the medicine—up to 20 pills a day—can ruin the treatment. Also at high risk of failure are those who were on other AIDS drugs, or whose T-cell counts were very low, before starting protease inhibitors.

The data from the real-world trial is less promising than information from carefully controlled drug experiments sponsored by pharmaceutical companies. In the longest-running of these studies, virus levels remain undetectable in 22 of 28 patients (79 percent) on the three-drug combination therapy. However, Deets noted that the patients in the study were less sick to begin with and they were more motivated to scrupulously follow their therapy regimen.

GENE RESEARCH AND HOPE FOR A VACCINE

Ultimately, the scientific community's goal is to produce a vaccine that protects people against infection from HIV. Vaccines contain some part of the virus, but in an incomplete or weakened form that cannot cause disease. This gives the body a chance to mount an immune reaction to the virus components without being in danger. Then, if the virus invades naturally, the immune system has learned how to ward it off.

Making a vaccine against HIV poses considerable problems, because it belongs to a family of viruses against which medical scientists have never made a vaccine. (In 1985 a vaccine was made against a retrovirus that infects domestic cats, but it was made in a way that would not be acceptable for humans.) Because it was only a few years ago that scientists found a human disease caused by a retrovirus, this is the first time they have tried to make a vaccine against a human retrovirus.

AIDS researchers are not just limiting themselves to the development and study of drug therapies. They are also struggling on a much different front, hoping to attack the disease on a genetic level.

HIV apparently has one major weakness: it can't reproduce on its own, but must rely on part of the body's immune system. It does this by altering the chromosomes of the cells it attacks, adding some extra genetic instructions that direct the cell to produce the special viral proteins HIV needs. Scientists hope to find a way to re-alter a cell's chromosomes, to either stop the cell from making copies of the virus or force it to make defective copies that would be easy to wipe out with other treatments.

Scientists have great hopes for this approach, especially after the summer of 1996 when research teams from the United States and Belgium discovered why a very small number of exceptionally lucky people are actually born with a natural immunity to the HIV virus. Apparently, in most people a single protein called a chemokine lodges on the surface of all T-cells. This protein (named CCR-5) is the gateway the HIV virus uses to get into the T-cell after it combines with another protein. In people with a natural immunity to AIDS, their CCR-5 is defective. In fact, they have a double dose of defective copies of the CCR-5 gene.

National Institutes of Health researcher Stephen O'Brien estimates that perhaps one percent of the white population carries this inborn protective mutation. Scientists hypothesize that the gene defect developed in some humans centuries ago to provide protection against a previous viral epidemic. A small portion of the black population displays AIDS immunity, too—yet the CCR-5 defect hasn't been found in these people, indicating that something entirely different prevents HIV from gaining a cellular foothold. Researchers now hope to identify new drugs that will mimic this effect.

The discovery of the defective CCR-5 gene and its effect on immunity could have tremendous implications for gene therapy and a vaccine—if altering a person's genes does not produce disastrous side effects. That research could take years.

But according to Dr. Flossie Wong-Staal, who led the gene therapy research in 1996, "It's no longer whether something will happen or not—it's more a matter of how long it will take."

Not all the news in the fight against AIDS has been as promising, however, especially on the vaccine front. Scientists realized early in the epidemic that it was too dangerous to develop a traditional type of vaccine based on inactive or weakened forms of the virus. They couldn't guarantee the virus would remain inactive once it entered the body, or that even in a weakened state it wouldn't have the power to eventually break down a person's immune system. In other words, scientists risked giving people the very disease they were trying to protect them against.

At first researchers tried what they called sub-unit vaccines made up of noninfectious parts of the HIV virus. That didn't work. Then they tried creating a hybrid virus by introducing a few HIV genes into viruses that are harmless in people, such as the canary pox virus which causes a rash when injected into birds but not when injected into people. Early tests in the fall of 1996 showed that some people did actually seem to build up an immune response to HIV with this vaccine, but more tests were needed to determine if hybrid vaccines were worth pursuing.

In September 1997, about 300 doctors and activists volunteered to be injected with an experimental AIDS vaccine made from a live but weakened strain of HIV. The vaccine was developed by Dr. Ronald Desrosiers of the Harvard Medical School, and tests with chimpanzees had been promising.

However, because the vaccine contains live HIV, there are some concerns that it could mutate and cause AIDS in the healthy volunteers. "I would not volunteer, and I'm not sure I would volunteer any of my patients at this point," said Dr. Margaret Fischl, director of the Comprehensive AIDS Program at the University of Miami's School of Medicine. "The concern, and justifiably so, is that this virus can recombine. Even a weakened strain can mutate back to a virulent virus that's fully infectious. The odds are low that it's worth the risk these volunteers are thinking of taking."

"There are going to be risks in a human trial," agreed Gordon Nary of the International Association of Physicians in AIDS Care, which coordinated the volunteer effort. "We don't know what the risks are. We can make some assumptions of what they are looking at in animal data. But we could be experimenting with animals for the next five, 10, 15, or 20 years."

The volunteers include people like Helen Miramonter, a grandmother and former nurse. "I'm 66, and a widow, so the decision was mine alone," she explained in newspaper reports. "I have lived a full and happy life. I hope to live a lot longer because I have a lot more work to do. But we've got young people, 15-year-olds, being infected every day. . . . I don't think people understand the profound effect of this epidemic."

Dr. Charles Farthing, the director of the AIDS Healthcare Foundation, was the first to call for human volunteers for the test—and volunteered himself.

"Yes, there is a risk that the weakened strain will chew up my immune system," Farthing said. "Yes, there is a risk that the virus could mutate and cause AIDS. What is the degree of risk? We won't know until we do the study."

It will take years of painstaking research to finally develop a vaccine that is even partially effective. The vaccine will have to counteract all of the known subtypes of the HIV virus found throughout the world. That's not counting the new variations of the virus that will probably develop before a vaccine is created.

ALTERNATIVE AIDS THERAPIES

In February of 1997, the National Institute of Allergy announced the development of several unconventional therapeutic approaches to HIV infection. One is whole-body hypothermia (WBH) which initial studies showed reduced the HIV virus level in four out of five subjects. Researchers say that WBH, if it remains successful, could enhance the effectiveness of existing multidrug therapies.

Another approach is PRO 367, an antiviral binding agent that scientists hope will use radioactivity to fuse genetically engineered proteins to HIV-infected cells to immobilize them.

An extract of the boxwood evergreen tree has been selected by the French Ministry of Health for evaluation as a natural antiviral HIV treatment, and large-scale trials of the extract were begun in 1996 at various medical centers in France in coordination with researchers in the United States. In a six-month trial of 332 HIV-infected patients taking the extract, known as SPV-30, over one-third of the patients experienced a decrease of more than 70 percent of the amount of HIV in their blood, according to the study coordinator, David Stokes of Brookline, Massachusetts, in a report he made at the 11th International Conference on AIDS.

The extract did not appear to be toxic and few participants reported side effects, he said. In addition, nearly half of all participants reported significant increases in energy level and in their overall sense of well-being.

Not all alternative therapies have the qualified approval of AIDS researchers, however. Some are completely ineffective and others actually are dangerous to the patient. These alternative HIV treatments include DNCB, a chemical used in processing color photographs; oral alpha interferon, which can cause flulike symptoms; Chinese herb mixtures; acupuncture; pentoxifyylline (a vasodilator); and "Compound Q," which is derived from the Chinese cucumber and can be fatal.

CHAPTER 9

PROTECTING YOURSELF FROM AIDS

"Each of us must realize that we are responsible for keeping AIDS out of our lives. We must learn about AIDS and must share what we know with our families."
— **Eric Engstrom**
AIDS Project Director
Minneapolis, MN

Call the AIDS Information line, 1-800-342-AIDS.

An Important Message from the U.S. Public Health Service
Centers for Disease Control

Our best hope for controlling the AIDS epidemic lies in educating the public about the seriousness of the threat, the ways the AIDS virus is transmitted, and the practical steps each person can take to avoid acquiring it or spreading it.

—*Dr. Otis Bowen, former Secretary of the Department of Health and Human Services*

Because there is no group of people who are not at risk for this disease—age, gender, sexual orientation, nationality, religion, or political orientation cannot exclude a person from being vulnerable to HIV infection—the most crucial line of defense against the spread of the AIDS epidemic is education.

The challenge of the public-education effort is to convince everyone there

A social worker talks with two male prostitutes about the dangers of AIDS.

is a risk of infection and to teach the public how to avoid the disease. As Dr. James Krajeski, a San Francisco psychiatrist active in AIDS prevention, wrote, "[A]ntibody-negative individuals can control their own lives and prevent the spread of AIDS if they avoid risky behavior."

Of all members of the general public, one age group is considered critical to the effort to prevent the spread of AIDS—teenagers. The number of AIDS cases that will exist 10 years down the road depends on whether teenagers today take personal action to lower their risk of being infected with HIV. The former U.S. surgeon general, Dr. C. Everett Koop, was particularly active in urging that young people be educated about their risk of contracting AIDS and how to lessen it. In October 1986 Dr. Koop said:

> We can no longer afford to sidestep frank, open discussions about sexual practices. Education about AIDS should start at an early age so that children can grow up knowing the behaviors to avoid to protect themselves from the AIDS virus.

Dr. Koop suggested that part of that education be explicit information at appropriate ages about how the HIV virus is spread by heterosexual and homosexual practices and by illicit intravenous drug use.

In order to know how to live safely, without generalized anxiety and unnecessary restriction of our lives, everyone should understand how the infection is passed, and recognize the physical realities behind those slick but vague phrases "intimate contact" and "exchange of bodily fluids." In brief:

- AIDS is NOT contracted by donating blood.
- AIDS is NOT spread by hugging, kissing on the cheek or lips, sharing cooking or eating utensils, or shaking hands.
- AIDS is NOT spread by tears, bedbugs, lice, mosquitoes, swimming pools, or toilets.
- AIDS IS spread by sexual intercourse—heterosexual or homosexual, oral, anal, or vaginal.
- AIDS IS spread from men to men, men to women, and from women to men during sexual intercourse.
- AIDS IS spread by sharing needles with infected IV drug addicts.
- AIDS IS spread to infants through the placenta before birth and through the mother's milk after birth.
- AIDS IS spread to health care workers through needle punctures.

That leaves two major areas of exposure to HIV infection—IV drug use or sexual intercourse. What can you do to protect yourself? What programs are being mounted to impede the spread of AIDS by these routes?

EDUCATING IV DRUG USERS

There are several ways to prevent the spread of AIDS among intravenous drug users. The ideal way, of course, is to keep people from using drugs. Prevention programs like the Just Say No campaign were initiated to help teenagers resist social pressures to take drugs, but they have had mixed success.

Also, treatment programs to help drug abusers "kick the habit" may help slow the spread of the disease. However, these treatment programs are too expensive for most addicts, and public funding for the programs has been reduced in recent years. Another problem is that while many addicts want to reduce their exposure to AIDS, they're not willing to quit taking drugs.

A highly controversial approach that is proving successful in slowing

AIDS cannot be spread by casual contact. However, an infected person can pass the disease through sexual contact.

the spread of the disease is needle exchange programs, which provide clean needles free of charge to IV drug abusers.

AIDS PREVENTION AND SEX

The methods of reducing or eliminating the risk of getting AIDS by sexual contact are simple. The safest approach to sexuality for adults is to choose either abstinence or faithful monogamy. If a person does have sex with multiple partners, that person must use a condom for protection. As Dr. Walter R. Dowdle, coordinator of AIDS activity at the CDC, said, "The message goes out for everybody that the healthy sexual style is the single partner."

For teenagers, the best advice consists of a series of options:

1. Do not have sex until you can form a stable and lasting relationship.
2. Engage in monogamous sex only.
3. Have sex only with people you know to be free from HIV infection.
    The potential embarrassment of checking this is worth it.
4. Always have protected sex, that is, use condoms plus a spermicide.

Although this advice sounds simple, there are difficulties complying with it. In particular, it is more difficult than it may seem to know

AIDS hotlines have been set up in many cities. More information about hotlines and support groups can be found at the end of this book.

whether a potential sex partner is free of HIV. A person may say he or she has had a blood test recently but be lying. Even a negative blood test from a few months or even weeks before does not mean he or she has not had sex with an infected person since.

A sex partner puts you at high risk for HIV infection if he or she uses IV drugs. But a former drug user could have been infected before stopping. If he or she does not tell you about a drug history, you might not know.

If you choose to have sex with a person, even though you feel he or she will not put you at risk of contracting AIDS, you *must* use a condom plus a spermicide. Birth control pills *do not* protect you from HIV infection, nor does an intrauterine device (IUD) or a diaphragm. Only a physical barrier to sperm or vaginal fluid can block out HIV. Latex

Until a vaccine for AIDS is developed, abstaining from sexual intercourse is the safest practice. Otherwise, condoms are the best protection.

condoms are the most effective. In laboratory tests they prevented HIV from penetrating. And latex condoms are more uniform in strength than animal-skin condoms.

Still, condoms are not foolproof. Some are defective when made. Some break. They must be used correctly and put in place before penetration. Condoms should not lull the user into a false sense of security; having multiple sex partners or failure to screen sex partners carefully will continue to pose a risk of infection.

Public-education campaigns against AIDS have been stalled by the reluctance of the mass media to present material using the word *condom*. It was not until early 1987 that condom ads began appearing in daily newspapers and magazines and on commercial television stations.

In November 1996, the United Nations joined forces with the

Chicago-based Female Health Company, a contraceptive manufacturer, to market a female condom to help fight the growing AIDS epidemic. The company signed a three-year agreement with UNAIDS "to provide a global public sector price for the female condom." Each of the 193 countries taking part in UNAIDS can buy the condom in bulk at a discount.

The condom is marketed as Reality in the United States and is priced at $3. It is sold as Femy in Spain, and Femidom throughout the rest of the world, where it is available in 14 countries. It costs $7.50 for a packet of three in Britain. The FHC said that by the end of 1996, 80 countries had already responded to the offer, demanding seven million condoms for 1997. The condom consists of a loose-fitting polyurethane sheath joined by two flexible rings. One fits inside the vagina, somewhat like a diaphragm, while another one holds the tube open on the outside.

TAKING CARE OF YOURSELF
IF YOU DO GET AIDS

The Agency for Health Care Policy and Research (AHCPR), an agency of the U.S. Public Health Service, has developed a series of pamphlets with the help of health care experts and consumers designed to help people cope with certain medical conditions, such as HIV.

One of the pamphlets, "Early HIV Detection: A Consumer Guide", advises that if you have HIV infection, you may feel, look, and act just fine. But you need to take good care of yourself as soon as you find out you have HIV, because this is the key to delaying the onset of more serious problems. Above all, see your doctor often; don't wait until you get sick. The following hints may help you stay well longer:

- Get immunizations (shots) to prevent other infections.
- Avoid exposure to infection—for example, people with colds or other illnesses, and human or pet waste.
- Eat healthful foods. This will help keep you strong, keep your energy and weight up, and help strengthen your immune system.
- Exercise regularly to stay strong and fit.
- Get enough sleep and rest.
- Finish your medicines, even though you may feel better.
- Worrying can lead to stress, and stress can weaken your

immune system, so take steps to reduce stress. Activities that may relieve your stress include breathing exercises, leisure walks, reading, and community activities.

- Hope is very important, so try to keep a positive outlook. Every day there are new drugs and treatments for HIV that may help you. Each time you visit your doctor, be sure to ask about new treatments and clinical trials (research studies) in which you might take part.

- You are not alone! There are a tremendous number of support groups and health care resources available no matter where you live. Your local library will have listings of HIV and AIDS organizations that offer support groups and counseling. Hospitals, churches, and the American Red Cross also offer programs and referrals. Newspapers often list times and places of different types of support groups.

CHAPTER 10

CONCLUSION

I n December 1996, President William Clinton outlined the official strategy for battling AIDS during the next four years of his term. In it, he offered six general goals—described as "simple, but vital"—to fight the disease that had become the leading cause of death for Americans ages 25 to 44.

The goals included: developing a cure and a vaccine; reducing and eventually eliminating new infections; guaranteed care and services for those with the AIDS virus; fighting AIDS-related discrimination; translating scientific advances into improved care and prevention quickly; and providing "strong, continuing support" for international efforts to deal with AIDS.

White House AIDS Policy Director Patricia Fleming said the strategy was not meant to address every aspect of AIDS immediately, but to act as a framework "that requires regular updating and adjustment as goals are reached and new challenges emerge."

Although the strategy did not lay out a specific legislative agenda or estimate how much money the federal government should spend on fighting AIDS, it noted that federal spending on AIDS research, prevention, and care, increased by 50 percent during Clintonís tenure, with $1.8 billion in Medicaid benefits going to HIV/AIDS patients in fiscal 1996.

Not all AIDS advocacy groups were pleased with the new National AIDS Strategy, according to a report by Reuters Business Briefing. "This plan lacks vision," ACT-UP spokesperson Steve Michael said. "We need a real national strategy, like what President Kennedy did with his campaign to put a man on the moon before the end of the decade."

Peter Piot, director of UNAIDS, the United Nations' AIDS program, used more urgent terms when he addressed the Fourth Conference on Retroviruses and Opportunistic Infections in Washington, D.C., in January of 1997.

"Only a vaccine can stop the AIDS pandemic. The epidemic is not over, despite what you may hear," Piot told delegates to the conference, which featured reports on the efficacy of new anti-HIV drugs. "I strongly believe that without a vaccine we will not be able to stop this epidemic."

Piot said that his speech was intended "to provide a reality check on our research agenda," because the epidemic is accelerating, not slowing down.

The AIDS death toll in 1996—1.5 million people—represented one-quarter of the total number of AIDS victims since the start of the pandemic. The reality, Piot said, is that it would cost $300 billion to provide the three-drug therapy currently recommended for treatment of HIV infection to everyone living with the virus. "Universal access to triple therapy is just not possible today," he said. "The current combination therapy costs 1000 to 2000 times the annual health expenditure per person in many African countries."

The global impact of AIDS has become more widely recognized over the past five years. According to World Health Organization and UNAIDS data through June of 2000, the reported AIDS cases since 1981 number 2,201,461 throughout the world—a number that most likely greatly underestimates the actual figure. It is further estimated that worldwide there are over 34 million people living with HIV/AIDS, and that over 5 million new infections occur each year.

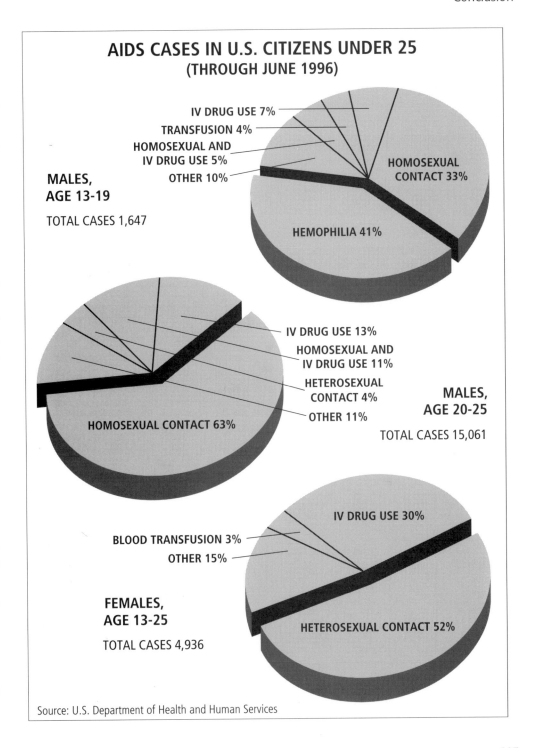

AIDS CASES IN U.S. CITIZENS UNDER 25
(THROUGH JUNE 1996)

**MALES,
AGE 13-19**

TOTAL CASES 1,647

IV DRUG USE 7%
TRANSFUSION 4%
HOMOSEXUAL AND
IV DRUG USE 5%
OTHER 10%

HOMOSEXUAL
CONTACT 33%

HEMOPHILIA 41%

IV DRUG USE 13%
HOMOSEXUAL AND
IV DRUG USE 11%
HETEROSEXUAL
CONTACT 4%
OTHER 11%

HOMOSEXUAL CONTACT 63%

**MALES,
AGE 20-25**

TOTAL CASES 15,061

IV DRUG USE 30%

BLOOD TRANSFUSION 3%
OTHER 15%

HETEROSEXUAL CONTACT 52%

**FEMALES,
AGE 13-25**

TOTAL CASES 4,936

Source: U.S. Department of Health and Human Services

113

The fear of a pandemic has become reality. The disproportionate number of cases in third world countries, specifically those in Africa, has made its way into the public consciousness. Sixty percent of the 16 million people who have died from AIDS since the 1980's lived in Africa, and the majority of the 9 million children who have been left without mothers or both parents also reside there.

Due to these staggering statistics, the Clinton administration designated AIDS a threat to U.S. national security in April of 2000, an unprecedented move. This is the first time that the National Security Council will be involved in the fighting of an infectious disease. The ability of the pandemic to destabilize nations economically, socially, and politically is a serious threat to add to the millions of lives the virus has already destroyed.

The search for a vaccine to prevent the spread of AIDS has been a top priority of private and public researchers, and new partnerships between the two sectors have increased the likelihood that a vaccine may soon be found. Merck and Co. has begun testing an experimental AIDS vaccine for safety in humans, a vaccine that reportedly prevented laboratory monkeys from acquiring full-blown AIDS.

There are as many as 35 prototypes undergoing human trials now, and hopes are high. The global strategy that Piot called for in 1996 to provide desperately needed drugs has begun to form. In March of 2001, Merck announced further reductions in the price of their AIDS drugs for South Africa, bringing the cost to only 10 percent of the cost in America. While it may be that legal battles and generic alternatives prompted the move by Merck and other pharmaceutical companies, the slash in prices is still welcome.

As the world moves forward into the 21st century, a vaccine and possibly a cure do not seem that far off. The death sentence of AIDS has been changed for many by the AIDS "cocktail," but the cost remains an issue. A willingness to work together and pool resources carries the potential to save a large part of the world's population from an early death.

FOR MORE INFORMATION

INTERNATIONAL ORGANIZATIONS

WORLD HEALTH ORGANIZATION REGIONAL OFFICES

Africa
WHO Regional Office–Africa
PO Box No. 6
Brazzaville
Congo
phone: 242-83-38-60
fax: 242-83-94-00
e-mail: afro@who.org

Eastern Mediterranean
WHO Regional Office–Eastern Mediterranean
PO Box 1517
Alexandria - 21511
Egypt
phone: 203-48-202-23
fax: 203-48-38-916
e-mail: postmaster@who.sci.eg

Europe
WHO Regional Office–Europe
Scherfigsvej 8
DK -2100 Copenhagen
phone: (45) 39-17-17-17
fax: (45) 39-17-18-18
e-mail: postmaster@who.dk

Americas
Pan American Health Organization
525 Twenty-third Street NW
Washington DC 20037
phone: (202) 974-3000
fax: (202) 974-3663

Canadian Society for International Health
170 Laurier Avenue W, Suite No. 902
Ottowa, Ontario
Canada K1P 5V5
phone: (613) 230-2654
fax: (613) 230-8401

Southeast Asia
WHO Regional Office–Southeast Asia
Health Services Department
World Health House
Indraprastha Estate
Mahatma Gandhi Road
New Delhi 110002 India
phone: (91 11) 331-7804
fax: (91 11) 331-8607
e-mail: postmaster@who.ernet.in

Western Pacific
WHO Regional Office–Western Pacific
PO Box 2932
1000 Manila
Philippines
phone: 63-2-528-8001
fax: 63-2-521-1036
e-mail: postmaster@who.org.ph

International Community of Women Living With AIDS
2nd Floor Livingstone House
1111 Carteret Street
London SW1H 9DL United Kingdom
phone: 44-171-222-1333
fax: 44-171-222-1242
e-mail: icw@gn.apc.org

Global AIDS Action Network
1931 13th Street NW
Washington DC 20009
phone: (202) 667-6300
fax: (202) 483-1135
e-mail: globalaids@aol.com

Global Network of People Living with HIV
PO Box 11726, 1001 GS
Amsterdam, Netherlands
phone: 31-20-689-8218
fax: 31-20-689-8059
e-mail: gnp@gn.apc.org

International Coalition of AIDS Service Organizations
Groupe SIDA Geneve
17 rue Pierre-Fatio
CH-1204
Geneva, Switzerland
phone: 41-22-700-1500
fax: 41-22-700-1547
e-mail: community98@hivnet.ch

Interagency Coalition on AIDS and Development
180 Argyle Avenue
Ottawa, Ontario
Canada K2P 1B7
phone: (613) 788-5107
fax: (613) 788-5052
e-mail: icad@web.net

United Nations USAIDS Liaison Office
20 Avenue Appia CH-1211
Geneva 27 Switzerland
phone: 41-22-791-4703
fax: 41-22-791-4162
e-mail: clarkm@who.ch

UNITED STATES
NATIONAL ORGANIZATIONS

AIDS Action Council
1875 Connecticut Avenue NW
Suite 700
Washington DC 20009
phone: (202) 986-1300
fax: (202) 986-1345
e-mail: HN3384@Handsnet.org

AIDS Research Information Center
20 S. Ellwood Avenue, Suite 2
Baltimore MD 21224
phone: (410) 342-2742

Centers for Disease Control (CDC) National AIDS Clearinghouse
PO Box 6003
Rockville MD 20849
phone: (800) 458-5231
e-mail: aidsinfo@cdcnac.org
CDC national hotline: (800) 342-2437

Committee of Ten Thousand (COTT)
918 Pennsylvania Avenue SE
Washington DC 20002
phone: (888) 488-2688

Direct AIDS Alternative Information Resources (DAAIR)
31 E. 30th Street, No. 2A
New York NY 10016
phone: (212) 725-6994
       (888) 951-5433 (outside New York)
fax: (212) 689-6471
e-mail: info@daair.org

Facts on Alternative AIDS Compounds and Treatments (FAACTS)
584 Castro Street, Suite 135
San Francisco CA 94114
phone: (510) 559-9448

Gay and Lesbian Medical Association
211 Church Street, Suite C
San Francisco CA 94114
phone: (415) 255-4547
fax: (415) 255-4784
e-mail: gaylesmed@aol.com

Harvard AIDS Institute
651 Huntington Avenue
Boston MA 02115
phone: (617) 432-4400
fax: (617) 432-4545

The Hemophilia Federation
918 Pennsylvania Avenue SE
Washington DC 20003
phone: (800) 230-9797

Hope Foundation
2212 M Street NW
Washington DC 20037
phone: (202) 466-5783
fax: (202) 293-9458

Lesbian AIDS Project
129 W. 20th Street, second floor
New York NY 10011
phone: (212) 337-3532

National AIDS Policy Office
750 17th Street NW Suite 1060
Washington DC 20009
phone: (202) 632-1090

National Association of People with AIDS
1413 K Street NW
Washington DC 20005
phone: (202) 898-0414

National Minority AIDS Council
1931 13th Street NW
Washington DC 20009
phone: (202 483-6622
e-mail: NMACI@aol.com

National Women and HIV/AIDS Project
PO Box 53141
Washington DC 20009
phone: (202) 547-1155
e-mail: womenaids@aol.com

Rural AIDS Network
1915 Rosina Avenue
Santa Fe NM 87501
phone: (505) 986-8337

Test Positive Aware Network
1258 W. Belmont Avenue
Chicago IL 60657
phone: (773) 404-8726
fax: (773) 472-7505
e-mail: tpanet@aol.com

APPENDIX

FURTHER READING

New books on AIDS are being published nearly every month. As the list of available books is too lengthy for this space, what follows is only a selection.

Barnett, Tony. *AIDS in Africa: Its Present Form and Future Impact*. New York: Guilford Press, 1992.

Bennett, Chris. *Managing Crisis and Change in Health Management: The Organizational Response to HIV/AIDS*. Philadelphia: Open University Press, 1994.

Hunter, Nan D. *Epidemic of Fear: A Survey of AIDS Discrimination in the 1980s and Policy Recommendations for the 1990s*. New York: American Civil Liberties Union, 1990.

Kirp, David L., and Ronald Bayer. *AIDS in the Industrialized Democracies: Passions, Politics, and Policies*. New Brunswick, N.J.: Rutgers University Press, 1992.

Kurth, Ann. *Until the Cure: Caring for Women with HIV*. New Haven: Yale University Press, 1993.

Leone, Daniel A. *The Spread of AIDS*. San Diego: Greenhaven Press, 1997.

Mann, Jonathan M., and D. Tarantola. *AIDS in the World: Global Dimensions, Social Roots, and Responses*. New York: Oxford University Press, 1996.

Norges, Rodger. *The Third Epidemic: Repercussions of the Fear of AIDS*. Washington: Panos Institute Press, 1990.

Rabkin, Judith G. *Good Doctors, Good Patients: Partners in HIV Treatment*. New York: NCM Publishers, 1994.

Rhodes, Tim, and Richard Hartnoll. *AIDS, Drugs, and Prevention: Perspectives on Individual and Community Action*. New York: Routledge, 1996.

Sepulveda, Jaime, Harvey Fineberg, and Jonathan Mann. *AIDS Prevention through Education: A World View*. New York: Oxford University Press, 1992.

Shilts, Randy. *And the Band Played On: Politics, People, and the AIDS Epidemic*. New York: St. Martin's Press, 1987.

Smallman-Raynor, Matthew. *London International Atlas of AIDS*. Cambridge, Mass.: Blackwell Publishers, 1992.

Weitz, Rose. *Life with AIDS*. New Brunswick, N.J.: Rutgers University Press, 1991.

World Health Organization. *Action for Children Affected by AIDS*. Geneva: World Health Organization, 1994.

In the United States, free pamphlets on various aspects of the AIDS crisis can be obtained from the Centers for Disease Control (CDC). Call their AIDS Clearinghouse at (800) 458-5231, the national CDC hotline at (800) 342-2437, or contact the CDC by e-mail at aidsinfo@cdcnac.org.

AIDS HOTLINES

Here are a few national numbers you can call for information:

- National AIDS Hotline (English): (800) 342-AIDS (2437)
- National AIDS Hotline (Spanish): (800) 344-SIDA (7432)
- National AIDS Hotline (TDD Service for the Deaf): (800) 243-7889
- National AIDS Clearinghouse: (800) 458-5231
- American Foundation for AIDS Research: (800) 392-6327
- AIDS Treatment Data Network: (212) 268-4196

If you have access to a computer with a modem at your home, school, or local library, the Internet is a tremendous resource for AIDS information and support. Start with the following. Each site will provide more links to other additional sites, or you can try using one of the Internet search engines to find a specific AIDS topic or group.

AIDS Virtual Library: http://www.actwin.com/aids/vl.html

AEGIS: www.aegis.com

ACT UP (AIDS activist group): www.actupny.org

CDC Gopher (The Center for Disease Control source for articles and reports): www.gopher://cdcnac.aspensys.com:72/11

AIDS in the News Media 1985-1996: http://www.kff.org/psr/toc.html

Journal of the American Medical Center AIDS Information Center: http://www.ama-assn.org/special/hiv/hivhome.htm

New York Times AIDS: http://nytsyn.com/med/Aids

AIDS Treatment and Data Network: www.aidsnyc.org/network/index.html

AIDS BBS Database: www.gopher://itsa.ucsf.edu/11/.1/.q/.d

Artists With AIDS Project: www.artistswithaids.org

COHIS HIV/AIDS: http://web.bu.edu:80/COHIS/aids/hiv.htm

HIV and AIDS Resources: http://ecosys.drdr.virginia.edu:80/aids.html

Queer Resource Directory: www.tcp.com:8000/QRD/aids

List of HIV-AIDS Internet newsgroup mailing lists: http://gopher.hivnet.org:70/1/newsgroups

List of other Internet AIDS links: http://128.228.5.100/aids/aidsrsrc.html

GLOSSARY

AIDS (Acquired Immune Deficiency Syndrome): an acquired defect in the immune system caused by a virus (HIV) and spread by blood or sexual contact. This defect leaves people vulnerable to infections and cancers that often become fatal.

Antibiotic: a substance produced or derived from a microorganism and able in solution to inhibit or kill another microorganism; used to combat infection caused by microorganisms.

Antibody: one of several types of substances produced by the body to combat bacteria, viruses, or other foreign substances.

Antigen: A bacteria, virus, or other foreign substance that causes the body to form an antibody.

AZT (Azidothymidine): one of the first antiviral drugs that was successful in prolonging the lives of AIDS patients; often taken in combination with newly developed protease inhibitors to reduce the level of HIV in an infected person's body.

Bisexual: an individual who directs sexual desire toward members of both sexes.

***Candida*:** a yeastlike fungus that often appears in people with AIDS; it causes infection in moist areas of the body, such as the mouth, respiratory tract, or vagina. Candida infection of the mouth is often refered to as "oral thrush."

CDC (Centers for Disease Control): A United States government-run medical and scientific center charged with tracking down the areas of origin of disease outbreaks. The CDC distributes literature and information on AIDS and is monitoring the spread of AIDS in the population.

CMV infection: An infection caused by a cytomegalovirus (a virus in the herpes family); severe infections can result in hepatitis, mononucleosis, or pneumonia. In those with normal immune systems these infections are usually mild, but they can be much more serious in patients with AIDS. Kaposi's sarcoma is caused by a CMV.

Condom: a sheath, usually made of latex, that covers the penis during sexual intercourse as protection against disease and/or pregnancy. Although a condom does not provide 100 percent protection against either, is it very effective when used correctly and in conjunction with a spermicide containing at least 5 percent nonoxynol-9.

DNA (Deoxyribonucleic Acid): genetic material composed of paired nitrogenous bases that contains the codes for an organism's inherited characteristics. Most genes and chromosomes are made of DNA.

Gonorrhea: a bacterially caused venereal disease that affects the genital mucous membranes. Antibiotics can be effective if the disease is treated shortly after infection; if gonorrhea is left untreated, however, serious complications may occur.

Hemophilia: an inherited disease, mainly striking men, in which an individual lacks adequate quantities of the substance that enables blood to clot.

Hepatitis: an inflammation of the liver usually caused by a virus and spread by contaminated food, drink, or needles. Hepatitis may cause the skin and eyes to take on a yellow color (jaundice).

Herpes virus: A family of viruses that contain large amounts of DNA. They include herpes simplex, which causes painful sores on the mouth (simples I) or anus and genitals (simplex II), herpes zoster, cytomegalovirus, and Epstein-Barr virus. In people with AIDS, these infections may involve greater areas of the body and be more persistent.

HIV (Human Immunodeficiency Virus): The virus that causes AIDS.

Homosexual: A person who directs sexual desire toward another of the same sex.

Hospice: A place specializing in treatment, both psychological and physical, of people with terminal illnesses.

Host cell: A cell on which a parasite preys.

HTLV: The first virus believed to be the cause of AIDS; however, further research disproved this theory and pointed to HTLV-III (HIV) as the cause of the disease.

Immune system: The body's mechanism for combating viruses, bacteria, and other outside threats. The immune system is composed of white blood cells (phagocytes) which consume bacteria, and lymphocytes, which produce antibodies.

IV (intravenous) drugs: drugs taken by injection into a vein. Heroin is probably the most common illegal IV drug. People who abuse intravenous drugs may contract AIDS through shared needles.

Kaposi's sarcoma: A formerly rare disease that commonly affects people with AIDS. This cancer of the walls of blood and lymphatic vessels usually appears as painless pink and purple spots on the skin but may also occur internally and involve organs.

Latency: ability of a virus to enter the body and then lie dormant for a period of time before it causes a clinical illness. AIDS has a latency period that may be as long as eight years, although more often it ranges from three to five years.

Lymph nodes: glands located in various parts of the body that filter microorganisms out of lymphs and produce lymphocytes.

Lymphocyte: a variety of white blood cell involved in the immune system. Includes B-lymphocytes and T-lymphocytes.

Monogamous: Used to describe a relationship in which the partners have sexual intercourse only with each other.

Neutralizing antibody: An antibody that coats a virus's surface and prevents it from entering cells. People with HIV do not produce neutralizing antibodies against this virus.

Pandemic: A sudden outbreak of infectious disease that spreads rapidly through the population, affecting vast numbers of people in many countries.

Parasite: An organism that relies on something else for its existence or support without providing anything useful or adequate in return. Parasites are often harmful to the host, as in the case of viruses.

Persistence: a term used to describe the length of time an infectious agent remains in the body once the disease has begun. In the case of AIDS, the infectious agent seems to remain for the rest of the person's lifetime.

***Pneumocystis carinii* pneumonia (PCP):** This type of pneumonia, or inflammation of the lungs, often affects people with AIDS. PCP is the leading cause of death in AIDS patients.

Protease inhibitors: Molecular compounds specifically designed to interfere with production of the enzyme protease in HIV-infected people. Because HIV needs protease to replicate itself, these drugs have been able to nearly eliminate the presence of the virus in some affected people.

Retrovirus: a virus containing RNA as its genetic material and with the ability to create a mirror image in the form of DNA. This DNA can combine with that of the host cell and allow the virus to reproduce. The usual procedure for viruses is for RNA to be created from DNA; therefore, this is the reverse. HIV is a retrovirus.

RNA (Ribonucleic Acid): genetic material composed of paired nitrogenous bases like DNA. Structurally, however, RNA is a single strand. The bases in RNA mirror those in DNA, enabling RNA to replicate its analogous DNA strand.

T-helper lymphocyte (T-4): A type of cell with a specialized function in the body's immune system. These appear to be the targets of HIV because AIDS patients show a strikingly low quantity of these cells in their blood.

Vaccine: A substance made of killed or weakened bacteria or virus that will stimulate the body to create antibodies against the disease caused by that bacteria or virus. These antibodies increase an individual's immunity to that particular disease.

Virology: The study of viruses.

Virus: A minute acellular parasite composed of genetic material (either DNA or RNA) and a protein coat. In order to reproduce, viruses must destroy their host cell. Viruses cause diseases such as polio, measles, rabies, smallpox, and AIDS.

World Health Organization (WHO): An agency of the United Nations set up in 1948 to coordinate international efforts in the health field. WHO, in cooperation with member nations, works to train health care workers, combat disease, and improve health.

INDEX

Abstinence, for AIDS prevention, 106
Ackerman, Gary, 38
Acquired immunodeficiency syndrome.
    See AIDS
Activism, 81–83, 84–85
Africa, 16, 47–48, 69
AIDS
    care of patients with, 71–72, 109–10
    cause of, 17, 51, 53
    HIV as, 15, 55, 56
    compared to other epidemics, 15
    costs of treating, 96, 112
    death rate from, 67, 69, 90, 112
    false accusations about, 73–74
    first U.S. cases of, 19–20
    latency period for, 53
    number of cases of, 49, 113
    official U.S. definition of, 62–64
    opposition to government funding for
        cure of, 81
    precautions against, 74–75, 103–9
    projected spread of, 16
    public denial of, 18
    risk groups for
        blood transfusion recipients, 40–41
        Haitians, 36, 41–45
        hemophiliacs, 36, 39–40
        heterosexuals, 37, 70
        homosexuals, 27–31, 70
        infants, 15, 36, 37–38
        intravenous drug users, 34–35, 37
        surgery patients, 36
        women, 36, 37, 38, 45, 70
    signs and symptoms of, 19–20, 22–26,
        31–32
    social upheaval from, 17–18, 73–75
    stigma of, 17–18, 75–77
    testing for. See Testing for AIDS
    transmission of, 18, 36–37, 104–5
    treatment of. See Treatment(s)
    U.S. strategy for battling, 111–12, 114
    worldwide spread of, 15, 16, 45–50, 69
AIDS Awareness Day, 80–81
AIDS Memorial Grove, 83
AIDS-related complex (ARC), 31
Antibiotics

discovery of, 14
in early treatment of AIDS, 20
Antibodies, anti-HIV, 58
Antigenic overload theory, 30
Armstrong, Donald, 21, 22
Ashe, Arthur, 79
Asia, 16, 45, 46–47, 69
As Is, 80
Australia, 16
Autologous transfusions, 40
AZT, 38, 89–90, 91, 95

Bacteria, versus viruses, 52–53
Bergalis, Kimberly, 78
Birth control pills, 107
Bleeding, as early AIDS symptom, 24
Blood
    AIDS transmission through, 36, 37
    screening of, 41, 54, 57–59
Blood tests. See Testing for AIDS
Blood transfusions
    in Africa, 48
    AIDS risk from, 36, 40–41
Bordes, Ary, 44–45
Bowen, Otis, 103
Brazil, 50
Britain, 48
Bruising, as early AIDS symptom, 24
Bubonic plague, AIDS compared to, 15

Canada, 16
Cancer, 31
    Kaposi's sarcoma. See Kaposi's sarcoma
Candida infection, 19, 87
CCR-5 gene, and immunity to HIV,
    99–100
Centers for Disease Control (CDC)
    accusations against, 73–74
    alerted of early AIDS cases, 20, 21
    investigate Haitians, 42
    purpose of, 20–21
    report reduced AIDS death rate, 90
    urge testing of pregnant women, 38
Children. See also Infants
    with AIDS, 15, 38, 45
    excluded from school, 18, 75–76

Clinton, Bill, 96, 111, 112
"Cocktails," in AIDS treatment, 68, 92, 95–96, 97–98
Communicable Diseases Control Act, 65
Condoms, 18, 46, 47, 70, 84, 85–86, 106, 107–8
    female, 109
Confidentiality of HIV-related information, 65–66
Counseling for AIDS patients, 38, 62, 65, 66, 110
Cryptosporidosis, as AIDS symptom, 25
Cryptococcosis, as AIDS symptom, 25
Curran, James, 27, 38, 53
Cyclosporine, 88
Cytomegalovirus (CMV), 20, 22, 25

Deeks, Steven, 97–98, 99
Dementia, HIV, 71
Desrosiers, Ronald, 100
Diaphragm, 107
Diarrhea, as early AIDS symptom, 24
Directed donation of blood, 40–41
Dowdle, Walter R., 106
Drug abuse, stigma associated with, 17–18
Drug "cocktails," 68, 92, 95–96, 97–98
Drug treatments. See Treatment(s)

Education about AIDS, 84–86, 103–5, 108
Elizabeth Taylor AIDS Foundation (ETAF), 85
Entertainment industry, AIDS awareness in, 79–81
Epstein-Barr virus, 20
Europe, 16, 45, 46, 48, 50

Factor VIII, for hemophiliacs, 39–40
Farthing, Charles, 101
Female condom, 109
Fischl, Margaret, 101
Fisher, Mary, 81
Fleming, Patricia, 112
France, 48
Friedland, Gerald, 33

Gallo, Robert, 55, 56, 88
Gays. See Homosexuals
Gene therapy, 16, 91, 99–100
Germany, 48
Gilada, I. G., 47
Gingrich, Newt, 81
Glaser, Elizabeth, 81
Gold, Jon, 21, 22

Gottlieb, Michael, 19–20, 21, 22, 30
GRID (Gay-Related Immune Deficiency), 31–32

Haiti, AIDS outbreak in, 42–45
Haitians, as risk group, 36, 41–45
Hemophiliacs, as risk group, 36, 39–40
Hensley, George, 42, 43, 44
Heroin users, 32, 34–35
Herpes, as AIDS symptom, 22, 24
Heterosexuals
    in Africa, 48
    AIDS in, 37, 70
    IV drug users among, 35
Hirsch, Martin, 92
HIV
    as cause of AIDS, 15
    early activity of, 94
    early care for, 109–10
    isolation of, 53–54, 55–56
    number of cases of, 16, 38, 46, 47, 69
    risk of, from sex, 107
    strains of, 70–71
    weakness of, 99
HIV-antibody test
    drawbacks of, 60
    ethics involving, 64–66
HIV dementia, 71
HIV Prevention Act, 66
Ho, David, 92, 94, 95, 98
Home HIV test kits, 60–61
Homosexuals
    AIDS in, 27–30, 70
    awareness of, 27–28
    in Brazil, 50
    change in attitudes toward, 83
    early AIDS cases related to, 20, 22, 31–32, 33
    in Europe, 48, 50
    Haitian epidemic blamed on, 44–45
    Kaposi's sarcoma in, 18, 23, 26, 27, 28, 33
    lymphoma in, 25
    Pneumocystis pneumonia in, 27
    reduced HIV-infection rate among, 16
    role of high sexual activity and AIDS in, 28–30
    stigma associated with, 17–18
Hospice care, 71–72
HPA-23, 88
HTLV. See Human T-cell lymphotropic virus (HTLV)
HTLV-III, 56
Hudson, Rock, 18, 77, 85

Human immunodeficiency virus. *See* HIV
Human T-cell lymphotropic virus
   (HTLV), 55, 56, 88

Immune system, 15, 19, 20, 22, 23, 26, 30,
   33, 51, 94
India, 16, 47
Indonesia, 46
Infants
   AIDS testing of, 38–39
   as risk group, 15, 36, 37–38
Intrauterine device (IUD), 107
Intravenous drug users
   AIDS in, 32, 34–35, 70
   in Europe, 48, 50
   needle exchanges for, 85, 86, 106
   prevention of AIDS among, 105–6
Italy, 48, 50
IUD, 107

Jaffe, Harold, 28, 90
Japan, 46
John, Elton, 81
Johnson, Earvin "Magic," 78–79

Kaposi's sarcoma, 18, 22–23, 24, 26, 27,
   28, 31, 33, 87
Kaunda, Kenneth, 48
Koop, C. Everett, 18, 76, 104
Krajeski, James, 104

Lamptey, Peter, 16
Latency, definition of, 53
Legionnaires' disease, 21, 52
Lymphadenopathy-associated virus
   (LAV), 55, 56
Lymphadenopathy syndrome (LAS), 31
Lymph nodes, 31, 94
Lymphoma, as AIDS symptom, 25, 26

Mann, Jonathan, 70
Markowitz, Martin, 92
Marmor, Michael, 28–29
McGovern, Terry, 38
Mellors, John W., 97
Memorial Quilt, 13–14
Memorials, 13–14, 83
Miramonter, Helen, 101
Monogamy, for AIDS prevention, 106
Montagnier, Luc, 55, 56, 88
Mosquitoes, AIDS and, 74
Mother Teresa, 72
Movies, AIDS depicted in, 79–80
Mycobacterium avium complex,

as AIDS symptom, 25

Nary, Gordon, 101
National AIDS Strategy, 111–12
National Institutes of Health (NIH), 52,
   53
Needle exchange programs, for intra-
   venous drug users, 85, 86, 106
Newborns, AIDS testing in, 38
New York, 67, 71, 72
Normal Heart, The, 80

O'Brien, Stephen, 100
Official U.S. Government Definition of
   AIDS, 63
Oleske, Michael, 37
Opportunistic infections, 22, 23, 31, 93,
   94

Parting Glances, 79
Pellegrino, Edmund, 76
Penicillin, discovery of, 14
Persistence of viruses, 53, 58
Philadelphia, 79–80
Philippines, 46
Pigs, AIDS and, 74
Piot, Peter, 45, 112, 114
Pneumocystis pneumonia, 19, 20, 22, 24,
   27, 31, 33–34, 39, 87, 90
Polio, 53–54
Portelli, Christopher, 90
Portugal, 50
Powell, Colin, 81
Prevention measures
   education about, 103–5, 108
   among intravenous drug users, 105–6
   public attitude about, 85
   sex and, 106–9
   success of, 16
PRO 367, as alternative treatment, 102
Prostitutes
   in Africa, 48
   spread of AIDS from, 35
   testing of, 64, 75
Protease inhibitors, 67, 90, 94–96, 98

Quinn, Thomas C., 70

Reagan, Ronald, 18, 64, 81
Red ribbons, as symbol of support, 86
Retroviruses, 55, 88, 99
Ribavirin, 88
Roueché, Berton, 14
Rubenstein, Arye, 37

Safe Sex, 80
Safe sex, 106–9
Saliva test, for AIDS detection, 61–62
Sandman, Peter, 17
San Francisco, California, 67, 71, 83
Saquinavir, 95
Sex
    AIDS prevention and, 106–9
    AIDS transmission through, 36, 37
    Sex education, changes in, 83–84
    Sexually transmitted diseases, high
        sexual activity and, 29–30
Smallpox, 15, 21
South America, 50
Spain, 48, 50
Spermicide, 107
SPV-30, as alternative treatment, 102
Stokes, David, 102
Support groups, 110
Suramin, 88
Surgery patients, as risk group, 36
Switzerland, 48

Tarantola, Daniel, 16
Taylor, Elizabeth, 84–85
Teenagers
    AIDS education for, 104
    drug awareness programs for, 105
    increase in AIDS among, 70
    safe sex for, 106
Testing for AIDS
    of blood supply, 41, 54, 57–59
    counseling after, 62, 65, 66
    ethics concerning, 64–66
    with home kits, 60–61
    in individuals, 54, 59–60
    in infants, 38, 39
    mandatory, 38, 39, 64, 76, 78
    reliability of, 60, 107
    voluntary, 38, 39
Thailand, 16, 46, 70
Theater, AIDS depicted in, 80
T-helper cells, 20, 51, 63–64, 94
Third World, unavailability of treatment
    in, 68, 69
Thrush, 19, 24
Toxoplasmosis, 22, 25, 87
Transfusions, blood. *See* Blood transfu-
    sions
Treatment(s)
    alternative, 102
    asking about, 110
    costs of, 96, 112
    drawbacks of, 15, 68–69

    early, importance of, 94
    early anti-AIDS drugs, 88–90
    failures of, 97–99
    gene therapy, 16, 91, 99–100
    guarded optimism about, 68–69,
        96–97
    improving access to, 114
    of individual infections from AIDS, 87
    protease inhibitors, 67, 90, 94–96, 98
    self-care, 109–10
    triple-drug therapy, 92, 96–97, 112
    vaccine, 54, 99–101, 112
Triple-drug therapy, 92, 96–97, 112
Tuberculosis, as AIDS symptom, 25

Uganda, 16
Ukraine, 45
United Kingdom, 68
United States
    incidence of opportunistic illness in,
        93
    quality of care varies in, 68
    reduced HIV-infection rate in, 16, 46
    spread of AIDS in, 70

Vaccine, 54, 99–101, 112
Vietnam, 46
Viruses, versus bacteria, 52–53
Visual AIDS, 86

White, Ryan, 75, 77-78
Whole-body hypothermia (WBH), as
    alternative treatment, 102
Wilson, Pete, 81
Women
    pregnant
        drugs for, 114
        testing of, 38
    as risk group, 36, 37, 45, 70
Wong-Staal, Flossie, 100

Zaire, 70
Zambia, 48
Zamora, Pedro, 79

PICTURE CREDITS

page

13:	AP/Wide World Photos/Ron Edwards	70:	UPI/Bettmann Newsphotos
14:	The Bettmann Archive	71:	AP/Wide World Photos
17:	UPI/Bettmann Newsphotos	72:	AP/Wide World Photos
19:	AP/Wide World Photos	73:	AP/Wide World Photos
21:	AP/Wide World Photos	74:	UPI/Bettmann Newsphotos
23:	U.S. Centers for Disease Control, Atlanta	76:	AP/Wide World Photos
		77:	Photo by Bob Durell
26:	AP/Wide World Photos	78:	UPI/Bettmann Newsphotos
29:	UPI/Bettmann Newsphotos	80:	AP/Wide World Photos
33:	AP/Wide World Photos	82:	AP/Wide World Photos
42:	AP/Wide World Photos	84:	AP/Wide World Photos/Ruth Fremson
43:	AP/Wide World Photos		
44:	Reuters/Bettmann Newsphotos	87:	AP/Wide World Photos
46:	AP/Wide World Photos	89:	UPI/Bettmann Newsphotos
47:	World Health Organization, Geneva	91:	AP/Wide World Photos
49:	Illustration by Sandra L. Taccone	93:	Illustration by Sandra L. Taccone
51:	U.S. Centers for Disease Control, Atlanta	95:	AP/Wide World Photos/CNA, Wang Fei-hua
52:	National Cancer Institute	97:	UPI/Bettmann Newsphotos
54:	Reuters/Bettmann Newsphotos	98:	AP/Wide World Photos
55:	UPI/Bettmann Newsphotos	103:	U.S. Centers for Disease Control
57:	National Institute of Allergy and Infectious Diseases	104:	Susan Farley/NYT Pictures
		106:	AP/Wide World Photos
59:	AP/Wide World Photos	108;	AP/Wide World Photos
61:	UPI/Bettmann Newsphotos	111:	AP/Wide World Photos/Joe Marquette
63:	National Institute of Allergy and Infectious Diseases		
		113:	Illustration by Sandra L. Taccone
65:	AP/Wide World Photos		
67:	AP/Wide World Photos		
68:	Reuters/Bettmann Newsphotos		

William A. Check, author of *Drugs of the Future* and *Drugs & Perception* in the Chelsea House Encyclopedia of Psychoactive Drugs Series II, holds a Ph.D. in microbiology from Case Western Reserve University. He is coauthor of *The Truth About AIDS*, which won the American Medical Writers' Association Book Award, and is a frequent contributor to medical reports for the National Institutes of Health and the Office of Technology Assessment.

Dale C. Garell, M.D., is medical director of California Childrens Services Department of Health Services, County of Los Angeles. He is also Senior Associate Dean for Academic Affairs at the University of Southern California School of Medicine. From 1963 to 1974, he was medical director of the Division of Adolescent Medicine at Children's Hospital in Los Angeles. Dr. Garell has served as president of the Society for Adolescent Medicine, chairman of the youth committee of the American Academic of Pediatrics, and as a forum member of the White House Conference on Children (1970) and White House Conference on Youth (1971). He has also been a member of the editorial board of the American Journal of Diseases of Children.

C. Everett Koop, M.D., Sc.D., was surgeon General, Deputy Assistant Secretary for Health, and Director of the Office of International Health of the U.S. Public Health Service from 1981 to 1989. A pediatric surgeon with an international reputation, Dr. Koop previously was Surgeon-in-Chief of Children's Hospital of Philadelphia and professor of pediatric surgery and pediatrics at the University of Pennsylvania. He is the author of more than 200 articles and books on the practice of medicine and surgery, biomedical ethics, and health policy, and received an Emmy in 1991 in the News and Documentary category for C. Everett Koop, M.D., a five-part series on health care reform. The recipient of numerous honors and awards, including 35 honorary doctorates, Dr. Koop was awarded the Denis Brown Gold Medal by the British Association of Pediatric Surgeons; the William E. Ladd Gold Medal of the American Academy of Pediatrics in recognition of outstanding contributions to the field of pediatric surgery; the 1983 Public Health Service Distinguished Service Medal; the Copernicus Medal of the Surgical Society of Poland; and a number of other awards. He was awarded the Medal of the Legion of Honor by France in 1980, and was included into the Royal College of Surgeons of England in 1982 and the Royal College of Physicians and Surgeons of Glasgow in 1987. Currently, Dr. Koop is the Elizabeth DeCamp McInerny Professor at Dartmouth College.